A Guide for Those Who Care About Creating and Supporting **Quality in Schools**

Leading After-School Learning Communities

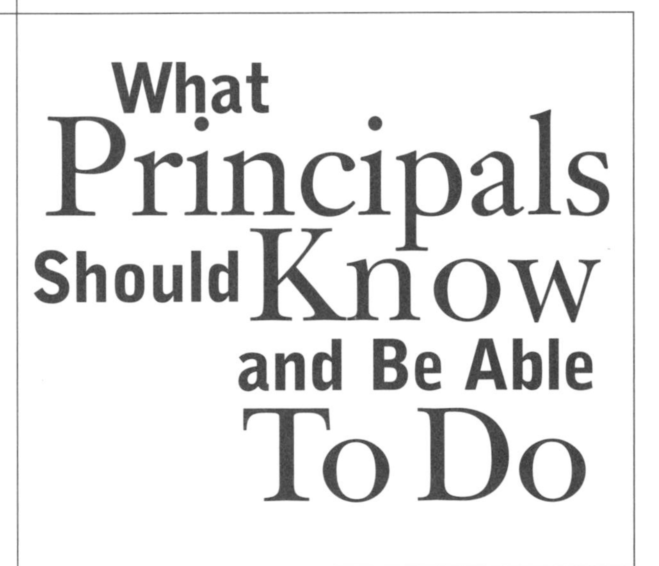

What Principals Should Know and Be Able To Do

NAESP National Association of Elementary School Principals

NAESP

Leading After-School Learning Communities was co-created by the National Association of Elementary School Principals and Collaborative Communications Group.

The research, development and publication of this guide were made possible through the generous funding of the Charles Stewart Mott Foundation.

Additional funds for this publication were generously contributed by Lifetouch Inc., of Minneapolis, MN, Paul Harmel, Chairman and Chief Executive Officer.

National Association of Elementary School Principals
1615 Duke Street
Alexandria, VA 22314-3483
Phone: 800-38-NAESP
Fax: 800-39-NAESP
E-mail: naesp@naesp.org
Web site: www.naesp.org

The mission of NAESP is to lead in the advocacy and support for elementary and middle-level principals and other education leaders in their commitment to all children.

The 30,000 members of the National Association of Elementary School Principals provide administrative and instructional leadership for public and private elementary and middle schools throughout the United States, Canada and overseas. Founded in 1921, NAESP is an independent professional association with its own headquarters building in Alexandria, VA. Through national and regional meetings, award-winning publications and joint efforts with its 50 state affiliates, NAESP is a strong advocate for both its members and for the 35 million American children enrolled in preschool, kindergarten and grades 1 through 8.

Collaborative Communications Group
1801 Connecticut Avenue NW
Third Floor
Washington, D.C. 20009
Phone: 202-986-4959
Fax: 202-986-4958
E-mail: info@publicengagement.com
Web site: www.publicengagement.com

Collaborative Communications Group is a strategic consulting firm that builds the capacity of individuals, organizations and networks to work collaboratively to create solutions that are better than any single entity could produce on its own. Through strategic consulting, dialogue and convening, creation of publications and tools, and community conversations, Collaborative helps organizations and networks to identify, share and apply what they know in ways that increase productivity and effectiveness. The ultimate objective of Collaborative's work is the improvement of the quality of public education and community life.

ISBN 0-939327-25-2

Contents

Foreword

By Dr. Vincent Ferrandino

When the National Association of Elementary School Principals released *Leading Learning Communities: Standards for What Principals Should Know and Be Able To Do* in 2001, we encouraged principals to take a fresh look at their role as leaders. More than ever before, we advocated for a focus on instruction and equity, offering support to principals in how they defined "quality" education for all students. We also promised that, over time, we would look deeply at new models of leadership and share effective strategies. Our intent was to help principals move toward new practices and behaviors that would help them create and manage innovative learning environments for students and adults.

Our commitment to expanding principals' thinking and practice continued. In 2004, with the release of *Leading Early Childhood Learning Communities*, NAESP encouraged principals to support an expanded continuum of learning, one that recognizes quality early childhood programs, principles and practices as the foundation for education. Acknowledging the important return on investment in the learning of children from birth through the primary grades, we provided specific resources to help principals create linkages between their schools and early childhood programs, whether these programs were school-based or school-connected.

Now, *Leading After-School Learning Communities* helps to expand the horizon for principals again. This guide goes even further than its sister publications. Thanks to the generous funding of the Charles Stewart Mott Foundation, a leading advocate for after-school programs, this publication will help make it possible to connect individuals, schools and communities. The strategies and resources in *Leading After-School Learning Communities* represent nothing less than the opportunity to re-imagine the learning day.

Focusing on the time children spend after school isn't new. Indeed, NAESP has a long history of involvement with after-school programs, beginning nearly 20 years ago with a survey of members who expressed concern for children's safety in the after school hours. In 1993, NAESP also created standards for quality school-age childcare and revised them in 1999. After-school programs have come a long way since then. Well beyond simply providing a safe place for children after the school bell rings, after-school programs offer vast opportunities to provide time for academic enrichment and support and recreational activities that children enjoy and learn from. After-school programs offer new strategies and opportunities to help children grow and succeed—in school and in life.

As the field of after-school matures, one thing is clear: After-school can no longer be an afterthought. Creating a seamless day—in which the school day influences the after-school program, and what is learned from after-school practices enhances the school day—is an exciting possibility to support children's learning. By collaborating with after-school programs and accepting them as vital partners in education, principals can advance their own missions and move closer to their ultimate goal of helping every child to learn and succeed.

Today, according to the Afterschool Alliance, nine in 10 registered voters agree that there should be some type of organized activity or place for children to go after school every day. Nearly three in four say that after-school programs are an "absolute necessity" in their communities. The annual survey is the nation's most comprehensive examination of the public's views on after-school programs, and its findings hold important lessons for educators, policymakers and families. Perhaps more than at any time in the past, Americans recognize that after-school programs help children learn, keep them safe and help working families.

The education community is also showing increasing recognition of the value of after-school programs. An NAESP survey released in 2001 showed that 77 percent of elementary school principals whose schools offer after-school programs said it was "extremely important" to maintain these programs. Nine in 10 rated their after-school programs as successful.

School board presidents agree with these assessments. Eight in 10 presidents in a 2003 survey conducted for the National School Boards Association said they had after-school programs in their districts and would like to see them maintained. The presidents gave the programs high marks for providing recreation, supervision and academic support. However, the board presidents cautioned that the continuation of after-school programs may be threatened by budget cuts.

Ensuring that all students achieve high standards will require the support of a comprehensive learning community that includes after-school programs. We hope this guide will help principals form effective partnerships that will benefit all of their students.

Dr. Vincent Ferrandino is the executive director of the National Association of Elementary School Principals.

In This Document:

- Principals see how connecting school and after-school adds learning time and helps create potential school partnerships. After-school programs offer learning communities a variety of tools to help students meet achievement goals. Principals need to have—and need to share with staff and the school community—a vision for how after-school time can complement the school day and provide new opportunities for children to learn and grow.
- Principals understand how to integrate after-school programs with the overall school curriculum and use after-school programs to complement, not imitate, learning offered during the school day. After-school programs can extend the learning day without becoming an extension of the school day.
- Principals learn how they can work collaboratively with after-school coordinators, without running after-school programs. Principals may not always have a hands-on responsibility for after-school programs, but they must work hand-in-hand with providers in joint pursuit of developing children.
- Principals envision creative ways to help children develop the critical skills and abilities that they need but that are often missing from the regular school day. Because of the emphasis on testing and achievement (which is important but has been narrowly defined), after-school provides extra academic help as well as opportunities to think, explore, create and perform in creative ways.
- Principals see how to use quality after-school programs as a way to connect students to additional caring adults and positive community resources, which add value not just to after-school programs but to the regular school day. Because after-school programs tend to be smaller and more flexible, community groups often see more possibilities for connection in after-school programs than they see with schools.

- Principals learn how quality after-school programs can be avenues to create stronger links with families. Studies show that parents and others who are involved in after-school programs have a more positive connection to schools.
- Principals understand how after-school programs can enhance academic support to students, by providing remediation, homework help, tutoring and mentoring. The programs offer academic enrichment activities that expose students to new ideas and information, enable them to practice their skills in hands-on ways and engage their minds, bodies and spirits.
- Principals consider different strategies for obtaining and sustaining multiple sources of funding to support ongoing after-school programs.
- Principals see how they can ensure program quality and evaluation. Principals can influence many factors that contribute to program quality and sustainability. These include providing adequate opportunities for after-school staff development, fostering a school climate that supports collaboration and helping to identify new and sustainable funding sources. In addition, selecting, generating and analyzing data about the quality of after-school programs can help principals assess the impact of programs and secure support and sustainable funding.
- Principals learn how to build relationships at the school district—and, in some cases, the state level—to advocate for systemic changes in policies and practices that can help create and sustain more effective and quality after-school programs and practices for all children.

How To Use This Guide

This guide is designed to help principals rethink the connection between learning within the school day and learning that occurs beyond the school day. It is important to note that while the primary focus is on programs that occur after the regular school day ends, the term *after-school* is used throughout the guide to connote learning that occurs during any out-of-school time, whether before school, after school, on weekends or in the summer. Such learning can occur in schools, in formal programs linked directly to schools, in community-based centers, in civic institutions like libraries and museums and in many other settings.

The guide is a resource to help principals and those who lead after-school programs reflect on their work and improve opportunities for young people. It is also intended for anyone interested in improving practice or policy related to after-school for students in elementary and middle grades.

Drawing on the work of principals across the country and the latest research on quality after-school practice, NAESP has identified indicators of what we believe constitutes quality in after-school programs. We also have defined six standards for what principals must know and be able to do to reach those indicators. The standards cannot be implemented piecemeal; to be successful, principals need to address all of them.

We designed this guide to be a practical resource for principals and their after-school communities. It offers practical examples, reflecting the work of principals who helped develop these standards. Principal and expert comments throughout the piece come from a group of principals organized for the creation of this guide. Each chapter includes stories of real people in school and after-school programs that exemplify the recommendations. Tools, examples and resources appear in boxes and sidebars throughout the guide to help improve collaboration of principals and after-school directors and the coordination between the school day and after-school time.

Several helpful documents have been included as resources and background. We realize our readers work in all kinds of schools, so we listened to principals representing a wide geographic and demographic spectrum to make these materials as useful as possible.

The guide has been designed to encourage browsing through sections and information, or to be read straight through. Whichever method you choose, here are some suggestions for getting the most out of the content:

- **Use it as a tool for reflection, particularly with your school faculty or staff.** Go through the list of practical guiding questions at the end of each standards section, either individually or with a small group at faculty meetings, with grade- or subject-level teams or in collaboration with after-school staff members. Encourage leaders of after-school communities to go through the checklist in each section to assess their own learning and plan next steps.
- **Read the profiles of schools and after-school programs and compare them to your own.** Study the two examples of effective practice in each section to see how to make a real difference in after-school. Look at the information on the demographics and context of the profiled schools to see examples that match your school community. See the problem, strategy or action the principal or school addressed in order to improve outcomes for young people—and the results of those actions. Look for examples that might help your staff and school community compare your current practice with desired practice—and identify the action steps needed to bridge that gap.
- **Dig deeper into a specific area of interest.** Study the important information on strategies for improvement in vision, community collaborations, infrastructure, linking after-school with the regular school day, evaluation and data and advocating for quality after-school policies and practices. Look at the suggestions for further research and resources if you have a particular area of concern, such as funding after-school programs or coordinating principal efforts with after-school program directors.

The Challenge:

Leveraging Learning and Community Resources

Children's minds don't stop when school ends, and neither should their learning.

Yet, in too many schools the bell at the end of the school day marks the time when learning does effectively stop, and children's minds, not to mention school facilities and resources, sit idle. Instead of enjoying a variety of engaging, fun and enriching learning opportunities, students face boredom or, worse, inappropriate behaviors that can harm them or others.

The need for stimulating places for students to go after school is particularly acute for working parents. More than 28 million school-age children have parents who work outside the home, and as many as 15 million children have no place to go after school. Two-thirds of Americans say that it is difficult to find after-school programs in their communities and that not enough programs are available. Many parents, law enforcement officials and community members worry that children aren't supervised.

But the potential opportunities for children after school go far beyond the need for supervision and childcare. The hours between 3 p.m. and 6 p.m. are a daily opportunity to support children's learning and engage their intellectual curiosity. And summers are times to continue learning and make sure skills do not slip. Many students need additional learning time as academic standards become more rigorous. The National Education Commission on Time and Learning's report, *Prisoners of Time*, stated more than 10 years ago that "if we genuinely intend to give every student an equal opportunity to reach high academic standards, we must understand that some students will require unequal amounts of time." The public understands this, too: In the 2004 Phi Delta Kappa/Gallup Poll, 94 percent of those surveyed supported increasing time for instruction.

After-school hours are a means of helping students, teachers and schools meet more rigorous academic demands. And they are an opportunity for tutoring, mentoring and remediating that can help keep students on track and in school, headed toward graduation. And they can do so in a fun, less pressured way that can be more engaging to students. At the same time, these hours are an opportunity for cultural, athletic, arts, music and other academic enrichment opportunities to engage children and broaden their interests. In after-school programs, children often engage in innovative, hands-on and experiential learning activities that are vital to the development of critical thinking and problem-solving skills. Particularly for schools that have had to scale back on arts-related subjects, an after-school program can help fill this void.

Principals across the country are encouraging the use of time after school for new and creative learning opportunities, offered in settings where children work closely with caring adults from the school system and the community. By most assessments, today's after-school programs make a positive difference in the lives of students *and* improve the climate for school success. And, because after-school programs offer a unique opportunity to engage the public and community organizations with schools, dynamic programs build public support that can advance a school's vision.

After-school programs are also popular with the public. A series of annual voter surveys conducted by the Afterschool Alliance shows public support consistently running in the 90 percent range, with 76 percent of voters even going so far as to say they would be willing to pay additional taxes to get more after-school programs.

Many principals see after-school programming as a means to address many of the vexing challenges schools face. With limited resources, personnel and facilities, principals are leveraging after-school resources to significantly increase learning time, while recruiting and rallying more allies outside of the schools to support expanding learning opportunities.

To advocates and practitioners, the benefits of after-school programs are already evident. Recent studies demonstrate the value of after-school—for students' achievement, social interaction and safety. Results vary somewhat from program to program, but the weight of the research is clear: Both in the short term and long term, in a range of settings, after-school programs done right enrich students, communities and schools.

Studies have found that after-school programs:

- **Keep children of all ages safe and out of trouble.** The after-school hours are the time when juvenile crime hits its peak. Children in after-school programs are less likely to commit crimes or to be victimized and are less likely to engage in aberrant behavior such as drug, alcohol or tobacco use.
- **Provide enriching experiences that broaden children's perspectives and improve their socialization.** Children in after-school programs develop better social skills and learn to handle conflicts in more socially acceptable ways. Children indicate they have higher aspirations for their future, including greater intentions to complete high school and college. Students who spend even one to four hours per week in after-school activities are 60 percent less likely to have dropped out of school by 12th grade than their peers who did not attend. Research shows that children who have the opportunity to make social connections in after-school hours are better adjusted and happier than those who do not have the opportunity.
- **Help improve the academic achievement of students who are not accomplishing as much as they need to during the regular school hours.** For many children reading and math scores have improved because of the additional attention spent on these subjects after school. Many programs provide more relaxed and enriching activities for learning, increasing students' interest in academic work and improving academic performance as well.
- **Are shown to be particularly powerful in improving children's interest and ability in reading.** Tutoring can lead to greater self-confidence in reading, increased motivation to read and improved behavior.

In addition, families with children in quality after-school programs indicate that their children are safer and more successful in school. These families also develop a greater interest in their child's learning. When families are involved in schools, students do better. Because they are smaller and more personalized than the regular school day, after-school programs offer more opportunities for children and parents to connect with other parents and families. And educators can also expect that when family and community members make an investment in an after-school program, they will be more interested and involved in their own children's learning, in the learning of all children in the program and in the life of the school as a whole.

Despite this evidence, the supply of after-school programs falls far short of the need. One recent NAESP survey found that twice as many elementary and middle school parents wanted after-school programs than were currently available. As many as 15 million children have nowhere to go after school, more than twice as many children as are in supervised programs.

Principals, struggling to manage the myriad demands of their own schools, are reluctant to add another responsibility to their plate. The goal of this guide is not to advocate for an after-school program in every public school or to say that every principal should add management of after-school programs to their already-full agendas. Rather, it's to show that "leading after-school learning communities" can support a school's mission and improve the climate for school and student success.

"Leading after-school learning communities" means that elementary and middle school principals should be at the forefront of discussions and activities that reach beyond the school to make sure that everyone involved in out-of-school learning—in schools or community settings—understands that a student's development also depends on what happens in the hours they are not in school.

By collaborating with after-school programs and accepting them as vital partners in education, principals can strengthen their schools and move closer to the overriding, common goal of maximizing learning for every child.

Principles

of Quality After-School Programs

Advocating for programs is easier if they meet certain standards of quality. The following is a summary of the principles of quality programs NAESP believes are necessary and aligned to the standards in this guide. The list is not meant to replace or replicate criteria developed by other organizations, nor is it intended to be exhaustive. Indeed, we suggest it as a jumping-off point for principals in their schools and communities to begin to define quality in after-school programs and as a tool to engage in conversation about the quality that exists in after-school programs where you live. How many of these principles are present in your school or community? What other principles might you add?

Quality after-school programs, whether they are based within schools or in communities, have the following characteristics:

Strong Vision, Management and Collaboration

Schools and after-school programs have a shared vision of after-school as an asset to the school. That shared vision is supported by communications that send the message that learning does not end when the final bell rings. Children are encouraged to pursue their own learning and set their own goals, and after-school is recognized as a different way of reaching students and helping them see the importance of education.

Intended goals are clear, and after-school programs have a strong organizational structure that combines hands-on, site-based management with regular oversight and accountability. Goals are established through collaborative decision-making and thus have a better chance of being achieved.

Programs also follow effective management procedures, including the use of annual operating budgets, accurate bookkeeping systems, affordable fee structures and multiple funding sources, including in-kind support. The administration focuses on the needs and desires of students, families and staff members and develops strong relationships with schools and community partners in order to sustain the program over the long term.

Sufficient and Quality Staff

Programs are staffed sufficiently to address and promote children's physical, social, emotional and cognitive development. Staff members are skilled, qualified and committed and have appropriate experience working with school-age children. Programs provide attractive compensation and work scheduling packages to retain quality staff. Programs use volunteers to reduce costs and the staff-to-child ratio, but they are incorporated into programs appropriate to their skill levels and interests.

Attention to Safety, Health and Nutrition Issues

Programs are safe and accessible to all who want to participate. They have adequate space for a variety of indoor and outdoor activities and age-appropriate materials to enhance learning. Programs provide a nutritious snack and other meals when appropriate, to provide time for relaxing and socializing and to promote sound nutrition for participants. Programs provide substantial amounts of health-enhancing physical activity and opportunities to practice skills taught in physical education courses.

Effective Family and Community Partnerships

Programs are designed with sensitivity to the schedules and requirements of working parents. They are affordable and provide transportation when necessary.

Programs communicate regularly with parents and provide them with opportunities to be involved in activities with their children. They also allow parents to make decisions and play an active role in leadership.

Programs use community resources effectively to provide long-term funding, facilities, materials, job shadowing, mentors, tutors and community service experiences. Programs include families and children in planning to garner support and develop activities that are fun and culturally relevant and that capture children's and adolescents' interests.

Enriching Learning Opportunities That Complement the School Day

Programs integrate their academic activities with those of the regular school to provide a continuum of learning for students. Programs offer academic enrichment opportunities that allow students to explore new ideas in new ways—through activities that may not always be available during the regular school day, such as art, music and drama. In that way, the programs complement the regular school-day program and meet students' social, emotional, cognitive and physical development needs.

Programs also offer challenging curriculum and provide support for academic learning by providing tutoring and assisting students with basic skills and homework.

Links Between School-Day and After-School Staff

Programs enable school and after-school staff to work together to establish and maintain relationships of mutual respect and understanding in an effort to maximize children's opportunities. Programs coordinate the use of facilities and resources to maximize learning opportunities and to prevent potential problems and misunderstandings.

Evaluation of Program Progress and Effectiveness

Programs are evaluated regularly in ways that incorporate multiple measures of success, reflecting program goals and avoiding single assessments that do not provide a full picture of learning or growth.

Programs have a continuous evaluation component built into the design so that program planners can objectively gauge their success based on the clear goals set for the program. In addition, pre- and post-assessments of students in the programs help identify where students are on state assessments and on teacher-generated assessments.

Staff members continuously monitor program goals, without necessarily using sophisticated research designs, in order to maintain their focus, improve effectiveness and accountability, ensure parent and participant satisfaction and identify necessary changes. Partners gather feedback regularly and systematically and use the data in decision-making around design and in making the case for funding to additional community stakeholders.

Defining Leadership in After-School Learning: Six Standards and Strategies for Principals

---

STANDARD ONE:
Expand the vision of learning to include high-quality experiences during out-of-school time.

STRATEGIES

- Demonstrate the belief that the school's mission, vision and plan encompass learning that occurs during and beyond the traditional school day.
- Articulate to all stakeholders the value of learning opportunities that occur after school, whether they are school-based, school-linked or community-based.
- Consider after-school opportunities as added learning time and a complement to, not an extension of, the school day.
- Extend the school's culture of adult learning to after-school staff members.

STANDARD TWO:
Act as a catalyst in the community to develop quality after-school programs.

STRATEGIES

- Collaborate with stakeholders to create learning opportunities for students beyond the traditional school day.
- Facilitate the development of an after-school plan that identifies and addresses the needs of students and the community.
- Connect students with a diverse group of role models who will help ensure their success.
- Encourage families to support and participate in after-school learning.

STANDARD THREE:
Collaborate with after-school site directors to manage resources that support the full learning day.

STRATEGIES

- Hold programs accountable to expectations jointly developed with the program director.
- Ensure that after-school programs are well managed and employ sound fiscal practices.
- Create formal and informal communication strategies between the principal and the program director and school and after-school staff members.
- Develop a positive culture between school and after-school staff members and mediate concerns when they arise.
- Provide appropriate resources when the program is implemented.

STANDARD FOUR:
Support linkages, connections and relationships between the school day and after-school learning that ensure program content meets community, school and student needs.

STRATEGIES

- Ensure that the school's learning and core academic standards are connected to activities in after-school programs.
- Offer learning opportunities in after-school that are different from, but connected to, those in the school day.
- Provide a continuum of services and supports for students.
- Connect professional development opportunities for after-school and school-day staff members to ensure consistency in standards of teaching and learning and to encourage relationship-building among staff members.

STANDARD FIVE:
Work with after-school directors to evaluate after-school programs to ensure they achieve defined outcomes.

STRATEGIES

- Define short- and long-term outcomes for after-school programs collaboratively with the program director.
- Use data to ensure that children most in need have access to after-school.
- Work with the program director to identify, generate and collect data to assess after-school programs.
- Encourage the use of data and best practices to improve programs by fostering communication about results among teachers, program directors, after-school staff members and other stakeholders.
- Use data and evaluation results to document program impact and make the case for quality after-school programs with school, community and political leaders.

STANDARD SIX:
Promote access to high-quality after-school programs for all children.

STRATEGIES

- Use the credibility of the principal to advocate for after-school programs for students.
- Understand after-school funding streams and policy issues.
- Keep the public and policymakers focused on the need for a continuum of services that supports students' learning beyond the school day.
- Promote and facilitate partnerships among schools, providers and communities that secure adequate, sustainable funding for after-school programs.

1 Vision

Expand the vision of learning to include high-quality experiences during out-of-school time.

Learning does not begin when the school doors open or end when the last bell rings. It is a complex process that evolves in different ways and in countless settings. Students spend only about 12 percent of their time in school. What happens during the hours when young people are not in a classroom has a profound effect on the academic, social and emotional development of children.

There is growing consensus that the traditional 180-day school calendar—a remnant of an agrarian past—has not adapted to the demands of a global society where young people are expected to have 21st-century skills that require them to be adept with technology, critical thinkers who can solve problems and continuous learners. Indeed, students have become "prisoners of time," as one seminal report from the U.S. Department of Education declared more than a decade ago.

An 8:30 a.m. to 3:00 p.m. school day is more ill-suited than ever to serve the needs of all students. During an era of rigorous federal and state accountability demands, students need opportunities beyond what the school day can offer to catch up on school work and accelerate their learning.

After-school experiences can be particularly effective in helping those students who may benefit from learning opportunities that may be in short supply in schools, such as personalized instruction, mentoring, tutoring and experiential learning. The social skills and self-confidence children gain from interacting with peers and adult role models are essential aspects of youth development. In addition, after-school initiatives present opportunities for enrichment activities and cultural programs such as art and music that are increasingly squeezed out of the school day.

Surveys show the vast majority of parents and youth want structured activities outside of school. African-American and Latino parents, whose children spend more time unsupervised than other youth, report an even higher demand for quality after-school programs. There is ample room for growth in this emerging field, which presents a window of opportunity for principals. Only 11 percent of youth in K-12 schools take part in after-school programs, according to *America After 3 PM*, a survey from the Afterschool Alliance. Some 15 million children, the Census Bureau and Urban Institute estimate, have nowhere to go after school.

Principals who expand the vision of learning to include high-quality experiences in after-school:

- Demonstrate the belief that the school's mission, vision and plan encompass learning that occurs during and beyond the traditional school day
- Articulate to all stakeholders the value of learning opportunities that occur after school, whether they are school-based, school-linked or community-based
- Consider after-school opportunities as added learning time and a complement to, not an extension of, the school day
- Extend the school's culture of adult learning to after-school staff

Demonstrate the belief that the school's mission, vision and plan encompass learning that occurs during and beyond the traditional school day.

Effective principals help shape a school's culture by setting priorities and expectations. By supporting a mix of complementary learning opportunities for all students, school leaders emphasize the importance of respecting these programs as integral to a school's vision for success.

Principals set an expectation for teachers, students and parents that after-school programs, summer learning opportunities, weekend enrichment and other quality out-of-school experiences are critical aspects of the learning process closely linked to a school's mission of helping all students achieve. These opportunities are understood to be as important as what takes place during the traditional school day and year. School leaders emphasize that after-school is a core part of a school's educational strategy. It becomes central to how principals understand learning communities.

Writing a mission statement that describes the goals of after-school programs can help foster respect for the importance of extended learning opportunities. Having an advisory committee made up of the principal, teachers, after-school staff, parents and students who meet occasionally to discuss the connections between learning inside and out of school can help establish a philosophy that recognizes after-school programs are part of a continuum of learning.

Inviting the after-school coordinator to sit on the school's management team can also underscore the message that after-school learning is vital to the school's mission. Such a step helps establish credibility for after-school programs and demonstrates that principals see a natural connection between the school day and what takes place after school. At the same time, by visiting the after-school program periodically, principals can convey to the staff, students and parents the importance of the program to the school.

Articulate to all stakeholders the value of learning opportunities that occur after school, whether they are school-based, school-linked or community-based.

While educators traditionally view the classroom as the central locus for learning, effective leaders convey a message that after-school programs are also learning-rich environments.

Principals tell a story about how after-school programs can help improve student engagement and attendance, address academic needs and offer new opportunities for adult role models to connect more deeply with students. They educate students, parents, teachers and community leaders about the potential for various after-school settings to help students. They recognize that the summer months, when many students backslide on progress made during the academic year, should be viewed as time when enrichment, tutoring and a host of other activities can support students' development.

Effective principals use data and stories from their own schools, along with national research, to articulate the value of after-school to school board members, political and community leaders, parents and philanthropic foundations.

Five Ways to Publicly Demonstrate Your Commitment to After-School Programming

1. Make after-school programs part of your school's vision and mission.
2. Include the after-school coordinator in faculty meetings. Schedule joint professional development activities that will benefit both school-day and after-school staff members.
3. Regularly visit the after-school program. Make it a point to stop by and talk with children and staff members.
4. House the after-school coordinator in a public location, such as the main office, school library or activity center.
5. Promote after-school programs to parents and the community through the school newsletter and Web site.

Regardless of where after-school activities take place—in school, in a program linked to school or in a community-based center—principals convey the message that consistent participation in after-school programs can:

- Improve attendance rates and deepen student engagement
- Provide all students with learning activities not available during the school day
- Lead to higher aspirations for students and help prevent negative social behaviors

In Boston, Citizen Schools, a local organization, operates after-school and summer enrichment programs for elementary and middle schools that give students the chance to apprentice with volunteer professionals. Students work with mentors to design Web pages, to learn about arguing a legal case or to write and design a book. In addition to learning new skills, students develop relationships with adults and see how lessons from school can be applied in a practical setting.

Consider after-school opportunities as added learning time and a complement to, not an extension of, the school day.

Principals acknowledge that after-school initiatives provide a unique setting for learning, engagement and enrichment. Quality after-school programs do not simply provide additional school, or offer more of the same activities in a different setting.

The culture of after-school environments provides for a more flexible, student-centered approach to learning that is distinct in style and structure from that of the school day. An after-school cooking club, for example, may incorporate math skills that reinforce concepts students are learning in class, but it is primarily a fun activity that exposes students to lessons about nutrition. A book club can offer students help with reading and grammar instruction that may be connected to English class, while at the same time providing them the freedom to think creatively about literature in a supportive environment.

FOCUS ON PRACTICE

Finding After-School Programs That Share Your School's Mission

Tom Archuleta, Principal
Valdez Elementary School, Denver, Colorado

When Tom Archuleta arrived at Valdez Elementary School—an urban school of 450 students located in North Denver, where 98 percent of students qualify for free and reduced-price lunch—he encountered a wide variety of after-school programs, run by community agencies, for-profit groups and parent volunteers.

In the absence of a full-time after-school coordinator or the funding to hire one, Archuleta initially assumed responsibility for coordinating the programs himself. He discovered quickly that many of the programs were poorly run and that there was little quality control. Providers, for example, would fail to show up and students would be left in the school building without supervision.

"Providers were taking advantage of us," Archuleta says. "They received grants or other funding to carry out their programs, and then looked for high-poverty sites to house those programs. Students' real needs often ended up being secondary."

Archuleta worked to change the way after-school worked at Valdez. He streamlined the school's after-school offerings, finding programs that complemented the school curriculum.

Denver SCORES, a soccer and writing program, for example, adds to Valdez's focus on literacy and also offers opportunities for students to learn to play soccer while they participate in poetry slams and community action projects. The writing portion of the program is particularly valuable for Valdez's bilingual population—96 percent of the school's students are Latino and 70 percent of students speak Spanish at home. The teachers enjoy the extra compensation the program provides, and they also benefit from participating in Denver SCORES literacy training.

Today, Valdez's after-school programs—which include the Scouts, individualized tutoring, Denver SCORES and other community-based programs—serve approximately 200 students. Archuleta now requires a firm commitment from each after-school partner. Providers are expected to assign a coordinator for their program, find substitutes when staff members are absent and be responsible for children in their care. Coordinators check in regularly with Archuleta, updating him on students' work and discussing the ways in which various programs are linked to the school curricula.

"Now our after-school programs really enhance what we do during the school day," notes Archuleta. "They share our vision."

"I would like to see principals in districts embrace after-school not as a stepchild but as a valued partner."

Carter Savage
Boys & Girls Clubs of America

After-school activities do not have to be self-consciously academic to help students learn skills that are applicable in school or deepen their connection with the school community. Research demonstrates that students who are involved with sports, after-school clubs and other structured activities with supportive adults have more success during the school day than their less active peers.

Most parents and students expect after-school programs to be different than the school day. According to *All Work and No Play?*, a Public Agenda survey that analyzed students' and parents' ideas about out-of-school time, even among parents who believe that public schools are raising academic expectations for students, only 14 percent say the best reason for youth to be involved in after-school activities is to improve academics. More than half of the parents surveyed agreed that young people get more than enough academics during the school and agreed that after-school initiatives should focus more broadly on activities that capture students' interests.

ARE YOU READY?

Questions to Consider as You Develop an After-School Program at Your School

Is there a need for the program? Have you surveyed parents and teachers? Are there other after-school programs in your community to which you might refer parents and students? Do you have an after-school advisory committee? (Committee members could be drawn from your site-based management team, interested parents and teachers.)

What are your objectives for the program? To provide after-school care for working parents? To offer additional enrichment activities, such as arts and music? To broaden students' learning opportunities and improve academic achievement?

Whom will your program serve? All students? Students in need of extra assistance? Children of working parents? Family and community members?

How will you structure your program? Will you partner with a community-based organization or hire your own staff? What activities will you offer?

Where will you house your program? Where will activities occur? Will you provide office space for a coordinator and other necessary staff?

How will you pay for your program? What will it cost? Will you charge families a fee? Will you apply for grants or use district funds? How will you sustain your program over time?

How will you evaluate your program's effectiveness?

How will you integrate your program into your school's vision and mission? How will you "sell" it to your staff? To students? To parents and community members? To your district?

FOCUS ON PRACTICE

Building on a School's Vision for Student Success

Paul Young, Executive Director

West After School Center, Lancaster, Ohio

In 1997, a community member approached Paul Young, then principal of West Elementary in Lancaster, looking for ways to help the school. Young knew students would benefit from one-on-one literacy instruction with a caring adult. But he also knew that when children are tutored during the school day, they miss out on valuable lessons in the classroom. Young asked the community member to come back—after school—to read with struggling students.

The volunteer did come back, and he brought others with him. A small group sat with Young in the principal's office and discussed the school's vision of learning for the 425 elementary students. They then talked about what they could do to build on that vision. They wanted the children to be encouraged and supported in their critical elementary years so that they could enjoy school, succeed academically, graduate from high school and become responsible adults who contribute to the community.

By the time that meeting finished, the idea for an after-school program was hatched. The program drew on the experiences and resources of a ready supply of local volunteers. Twenty low-performing students were identified and matched with 20 adults. The pairs began meeting in a nearby church for tutoring after school hours.

Young and the volunteers knew that what they were accomplishing in the after-school program was important to students, families and the community. But they also knew it wasn't quite enough. To reach their vision, they needed to offer additional supports—especially to the 65 percent of students who qualified for free and reduced-price lunch at the school.

Young began meeting with key stakeholders to communicate the importance of tutoring and mentoring programs, health and social supports, recreational and arts opportunities and safe environments for students. He started writing grant proposals to the city and local and state agencies to secure funding for program expansion. He used grant money to hire a coordinator, who took over responsibilities for program content, organization and materials. He facilitated conversations with community members that led to the incorporation of the program and helped form a board of directors that worked to carry out its mission.

The newly formed organization, West After School Center, purchased a city lot adjacent to the school. In 2003, the West After School Center opened its new facility's doors.

Although the program and the school are now officially separate entities, it still maintains its original goal of enhancing student learning and helping all children graduate. Nearly 20 percent of West Elementary's student population is currently enrolled in the after-school program, and all students are welcome to partake in the center's activities or to access resources.

The West After School Center has received positive media attention for its music, art, drama, recreational, academic, early childhood and adult learning opportunities, as well as its effective engagement of local volunteers. The center is still closely linked with the school; school staff members help identify and enroll at-risk students who would most benefit from the program. The center also supports the school with conflict management facilitation and by offering professional development opportunities to school and after-school staff.

Young still believes after-school is essential to student success. When he retired from his principalship in December 2004, he became the executive director of the West After School Center. In this new capacity, Young continues to build partnerships with local agencies, evaluate and improve programming, foster ownership and buy-in from the community and secure funding that will help sustain both the program and the shared vision and mission for West Elementary School.

Young people concur. They need room to grow, play, take risks and make mistakes. The emphasis on high-stakes exams that increasingly begin at earlier grades makes it harder for children to have those spontaneous opportunities in school. After-school programs can help fill that gap. By incorporating youth voice in the design of after-school programs, principals can ensure that the kinds of activities youths want—and that they will participate in—actually get created.

"Principals need to help teachers see the connections—after-school helps students do better in the school."

Tom Archuleta, Principal Valdez Elementary School Denver, Colorado

In New York City, community centers called Beacons are located inside public schools and offer a range of recreational, academic and cultural enrichment activities before and after school, as well as on the weekends and in the evenings. Nearly 90 percent of the Beacons have a youth council that helps make decisions about what the program will look like and three-quarters of them engage youth as paid staff.

Extend the school's culture of adult learning to after-school staff members.

Successful principals seek opportunities to provide teachers with time to develop new skills. In some cases, however, school leaders overlook the contributions of after-school staff members and rarely include them in this culture of adult learning.

Teachers and after-school staff members learn to respect and value each other when they are encouraged to reflect on the similarities and differences in their work. They begin to appreciate the need to work more closely when they are given shared time to discuss challenges, compare teaching styles, coordinate mutual goals and learn together.

Principals emphasize that after-school staff members should be considered equal partners who bring a valued set of skills and experiences to educating young people. By encouraging a collaborative dynamic, principals help better prepare school and after-school staff to become more responsive and effective educators. Principals should consider inviting after-school staff to teacher training seminars and regular staff meetings and seek out opportunities for teachers to observe after-school activities.

QUESTIONS FOR FURTHER REFLECTION

Demonstrate the belief that the school's mission, vision and plan encompass learning that occurs during and beyond the traditional school day.

- Is the importance of after-school learning reflected in our school's mission statement?
- Is the importance reflected in my vision and plan for the school?
- How do I demonstrate my commitment to learning both during and after school?
- Do I share school resources with the after-school program?
- Do I include school and after-school staff on curriculum planning committees?
- Is there an after-school representative on our site-based management team?

Articulate to all stakeholders the value of learning opportunities that occur after-school, whether they are school-based, school-linked or community-based.

- Am I familiar with the research on after-school learning?
- How do I articulate the value of after-school learning opportunities?
- Do I underscore the importance of after-school learning in meetings I have with parents? Administrators? Students?
- Do I include references to after-school learning in the school newsletter and Web site?

Consider after-school opportunities as added learning time and a complement to, not an extension of, the school day.

- What type of activities does our after-school program include?
- How do those activities complement, yet differ from, activities students participate in during school?
- Are there a variety of offerings?
- Do students see after-school as fun?
- Do they have a voice in helping determine which activities will be offered and how they will be structured?

Extend the school's culture of adult learning to after-school staff members.

- Do school and after-school staff members work cooperatively together?
- Do I include after-school staff members in school-based professional development?
- Do I look for ways to include school staff members in staff development opportunities for after-school staff members?

PLANNING TOOL

This assessment is designed to help you and your leadership team periodically reflect on your school practice. Look back at your answers to the Questions for Further Reflection as you complete this assessment. Take the assessment at the beginning, middle and end of the year to track your progress. Note things you are doing well or want to change.

Once you have mastered an item, shift your focus to other items. You may add to the assessment if you discover additional indicators you would like to track. If a question is not applicable, leave it blank. Rate each question from 1 to 4: **1** Not at all, **2** Sometimes, **3** Most of the time, **4** Always

Demonstrate the belief that the school's mission, vision and plan encompass learning that occurs during and beyond the traditional school day.	Beginning Rating	Middle Rating	End Rating
The importance of after-school learning is reflected in my vision and plan for the school.			
School and after-school programs share resources.			
School and after-school staff members are included on curriculum planning committees.			
There is an after-school representative on my school's site-based management team.			
Articulate to all stakeholders the value of learning opportunities that occur after-school, whether they are school-based, school-linked or community-based.			
I emphasize the importance of after-school learning in:			
meetings with parents			
meetings with administrators			
meetings with students			
meetings with community members			
References to after-school learning are included in:			
the school newsletter			
the school Web site			

Consider after-school opportunities as added learning time and a complement to, not an extension of, the school day.	Beginning Rating	Middle Rating	End Rating
Our after-school program offers a variety of activities.			
Activities are different from school-day activities.			
After-school activities complement in-school activities.			
Students have input into which after-school activities will be offered and how they will be structured.			

Extend the school's culture of adult learning to after-school staff members.			
There are ample opportunities for school and after-school staff members to learn from each other.			
School and after-school staff members work cooperatively together.			
After-school staff members are viewed as respected educators by our school community.			
After-school staff members are included in school-based professional development activities.			
School staff members are included in staff development opportunities for after-school staff.			

NOTES

FOR MORE INFORMATION

Resources From NAESP

Magnuson, P. "Extending the Day: School Programs Fill the Void Before and After-School." *Communicator*, March 2001.

National Association of Elementary School Principals. "Principals and After-School Programs: A Survey of K-8 Principals." Fact sheet, 2001.

On the Web

Center for Summer Learning (www.summerlearning.org) at Johns Hopkins University develops, evaluates and disseminates model summer learning programs; stimulates research; and builds public support to ensure that all children have access to learning opportunities during the summer months.

Citizen Schools (www.citizenschools.org) operates a network of after-school and summer enrichment programs for elementary and middle schools that give students the chance to apprentice with volunteer professionals.

Collaborative Communications Group offers Resources on Afterschool (www.publicengagement.com/AfterschoolResources/), an online library that contains a plethora of after-school tools, guides and research on policy, legislation, financing strategies, outreach, research and quality.

National Youth Development Information Center (www.nydic.org) serves as a clearinghouse of resources on funding, staffing, programming, research and advocacy.

Program in Afterschool Education and Research (www.gse.harvard.edu/~afterschool) is dedicated to making meaningful theoretical and practical contributions to the field of after-school. Its publication "New Directions for Youth Development" gives valuable practitioner perspectives on after-school.

From the Research

Afterschool Investments Project. *Creating a Vision for Afterschool Partnerships.* Washington, DC: U.S. Department of Health and Human Services, 2004.

The Annie E. Casey Foundation. *Success in School: Education Ideas That Count.* Baltimore, MD: 2005.

Duffett, A. and Johnson, J. *All Work and No Play? Listening to What Kids and Parents Really Want From Out-of-School Time.* New York: Public Agenda, 2004.

The Finance Project. *Creating a Vision for After School Partnerships.* Washington, DC: June 2004.

National Education Commission on Time and Learning. *Prisoners of Time.* Washington, DC: U.S. Department of Education, 1994.

U.S. Department of Education. *After-School Programs: Keeping Children Safe and Smart.* Washington, DC: 2000.

2

Community Catalyst

Act as a catalyst in the community to develop quality after-school programs

Schools do not exist in a vacuum. Their vitality and success are linked to the communities of which they are a part. Principals recognize this symbiotic relationship and reach out to establish networks with other community leaders who have an interest in the positive development of young people.

Students, too, understand the need to connect with the community outside of school. They yearn to make connections with supportive adults, deepen community bonds and feel they are part of a thriving civic culture.

After-school can become a center of community life, a renewed public square where children and adults gather to learn, play and grow together. At their best, after-school programs become sources of civic pride that have the potential to strengthen community engagement and create safer and stronger neighborhoods. They become a point of connection for schools, families and communities. The burgeoning community schools movement, which is often characterized by strong after-school programs, is perhaps the best example of how schools are forging links to the community. These "full service" schools are open from early in the morning until late in the evening and provide programs to students and adults on weekends and in the summer. They have become one-stop shopping for health care, employment training, counseling services and a host of other support systems for young people and their families.

Principals have the credibility to initiate conversations about the value of after-school programs with community-based organizations, colleges and universities, business groups and social service providers. These stakeholders are often eager to collaborate with schools to develop after-school and summer enrichment programs. Principals recognize that they are well positioned to bring these partners to the table and communicate the ways that after-school can enhance students' development and well being. Together, principals and their partners can explore opportunities, discuss challenges and develop strategies for more effectively supporting students when they are not in school.

Principals who act as a catalyst in the community to develop high-quality after-school programs:

- Collaborate with stakeholders to create learning opportunities for students beyond the traditional school day
- Facilitate the development of an after-school plan that identifies and addresses the needs of students and the community
- Connect students with a diverse group of role models who will help ensure their success
- Encourage families to support and participate in after-school learning

Collaborate with stakeholders to create learning opportunities for students beyond the traditional school day.

Principals are community leaders with respected voices who motivate, persuade, build alliances and use leverage to improve conditions for students' success.

They are most successful in ensuring meaningful after-school opportunities for students when they work together with other community partners and embrace a philosophy of shared leadership.

Effective principals look to colleges and universities, local social service providers, faith-based organizations and business leaders to help develop after-school opportunities for all students. This process of engagement is best reflected in a leadership style that understands the importance of transcending institutional boundaries and seeking consensus about how to best serve young people.

When schools work together with community groups and other organizations, they tap into powerful sources of support. These organizations have often been serving youth and families for years and bring invaluable institutional resources. The partnerships that are formed also help schools by bringing new allies to the table and forging relationships that can become mutually beneficial over the long run.

In communities where after-school initiatives have been embraced in systematic ways by school and civic leaders, programs have been successful in bringing together an eclectic mix of government agencies, universities, businesses and nonprofit groups. By drawing on the resources and capacity of these institutions, principals improve the chances that students will have access to enriching after-school activities.

In Boston, the city's After-School for All Partnership casts a wide net by tapping government, corporate and higher education leaders to support a quality after-school system. Partners include the mayor's office, the United Way of Massachusetts, Harvard University, the Boston Foundation and Bank of America. For more information about the partnership, visit www.afterschoolforall.org.

The 6 to 6 Extended School Day Program in San Diego is a partnership between the city's community and economic development department and the city's school district. It provides academic enrichment, performing arts opportunities, homework help and recreational activities for about 22,000 elementary and middle school students. The city's police department reported that while there has been an overall increase in crime, juvenile arrests during after-school hours dropped 13 percent, and the victimization rates of juveniles during after-school hours decreased by 11 percent. The police chief specifically cited the 6 to 6 program for the improvements. For more information, visit www.sandiego.gov/6to6/index.shtml.

Facilitate the development of an after-school plan that identifies and addresses the needs of students and the community.

After-school initiatives will be effective only if they are responsive to students, parents and other community members. While best practices and standards for after-school provide indicators of quality programming, there is no single blueprint for what after-school should look like across the country. Programs will be shaped by the unique characteristics, challenges, goals and history of the diverse communities that come to define them.

An after-school plan that clearly reflects community expectations for after-school programs will help principals ensure the programs are relevant and meaningful. Principals should be as specific as possible about what types of programs will be most beneficial for their students and parents.

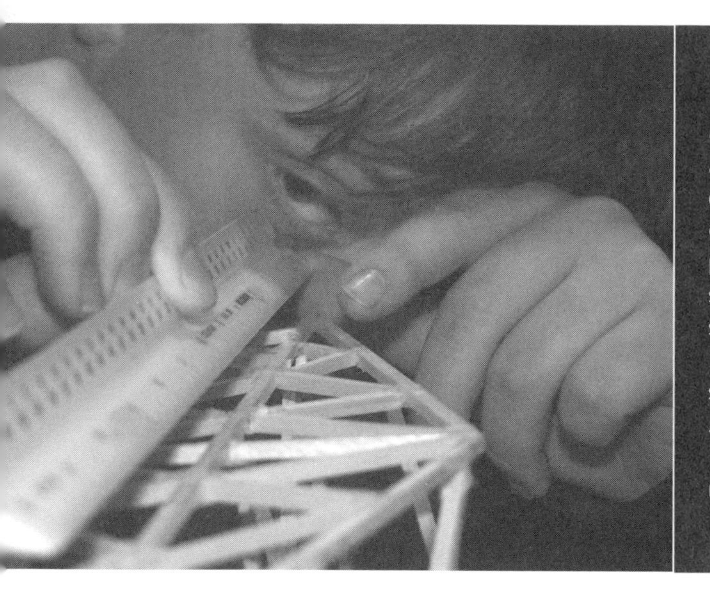

Consider partnering with a community-based organization to hold a forum on after-school activities that will help bring parents, students, educators and community leaders together to generate ideas and galvanize support for these programs. Information gathered from forums, surveys or focus groups could help inform the substance of an after-school plan. For more information about developing a community vision, see *Creating a Vision for Afterschool Partnerships,* Afterschool Investments project, U.S. Department of Health and Human Services, nccic.org/afterschool/presources.html.

An after-school plan can become a guiding document that can be updated, revised and used as a framework for thinking critically about after-school initiatives.

Principals and after-school directors who engage communities in planning for after-school initiatives:

- Have conversations with teachers, parents and other community members about how after-school programs can improve the overall quality of the school
- Assemble a planning team that broadly represents students, teachers, parents and community leaders to assess the needs of students and families
- Visit other schools to see what works in exemplary after-school programs

Connect students with a diverse group of role models who will help ensure their success.

When students have positive connections with adults, they learn in ways that a teacher's best lesson plan or a textbook assignment can never replicate. Having varied experiences with adults helps students see the practical benefits of education, inspires young people to think about future goals and broadens the network of adult support that contributes to children's success.

Principals should recognize the potential of after-school activities for providing a natural setting where adults and students can come together to form relationships. Principals can coordinate with the after-school director to invite a range of professionals with different backgrounds—doctors, police officers, carpenters, judges, teachers and political leaders—to visit after-school programs.

FOCUS ON PRACTICE

Community Efforts in After-School

Juli Kwikkel, Principal
East and West Elementary Schools, Storm Lake, Iowa

The faces in Storm Lake schools have changed over the past 10 years. A wave of immigrants, most of whom have come to the area to work at local meat processing plants, has led to an increase of students who are English language learners in schools—from 61 students in 1994 to more than 900 students in 2005.

Juli Kwikkel, principal of two of the town's elementary schools, knows student, parent and community needs are different from what they used to be. And she believes after-school programs are essential to meeting those evolving needs.

Funded by 21st Century Community Learning Centers grant money, Storm Lake's after-school programs are run through a partnership of local agencies and organizations, including CommUNITY Education—a city- and school district-funded network focused on increasing educational opportunities for the town's youth—Iowa State University Extension, local colleges and universities, a local AmeriCorps program and the Storm Lake public library.

Kwikkel works with the after-school program coordinator at the district level and site coordinators in the elementary school buildings to ensure learning opportunities offered beyond school hours meet the needs of students and parents. "School staff has the best pulse on what's happening with the kids and what their needs are. We are the ones who can best determine what will help kids achieve."

According to Kwikkel, city-wide partnerships and a community-wide focus on education have created high-quality after-school programs that help students learn, encourage parents to become more involved in schools and allow the community to embrace new residents and connect them to resources they need to thrive.

Storm Lake's extended learning opportunities offer 380 students academic assistance, including one-to-one tutoring; small group homework assistance; small group concentrated reading; math, reading and science activities; and summer school. Programs also offer educational enrichment activities including mentoring, character education, drama programs and service learning projects. Parents and families of students come to schools for monthly family nights, family math, adult GED and ELL classes and parenting courses.

Local businesses and organizations partner with the after-school program to offer students real-world learning opportunities that teach lessons of civic responsibility and social consciousness. Students in elementary and middle school after-school programs recently created a business plan, sold jars of soup and contributed their profits to the Hurricane Katrina relief effort.

Education students at local colleges and universities staff after-school programs, giving them valuable experience in the field and an opportunity to be involved in the community.

"These programs benefit the entire community," says Kwikkel. "Kids are getting their homework done, students and parents are learning the language while they learn about the school and community and the community is fully engaged in education."

Music education at the Sparta School, located in rural Alleghany County, NC, had been cut, but school staff members there found a solution: create a music program in the school's after-school program. They enlisted accomplished local musicians as teachers and bought guitars, fiddles and dulcimers with 21st Century Community Learning Center funds. Now the program, known as Junior Appalachian Musicians (JAM), has connected young people with the traditions of the community, as well as with parents and grandparents. Family music nights are now common.

A lawyer could help students set up a mock trial to teach students about how the justice system operates, while helping them sharpen their writing and speaking skills. A carpenter could teach students about woodworking and how mathematical dimensions relate to construction and design. A doctor can provide practical lessons about science, nutrition and the importance of exercise.

"We're looking for innovative ideas and trying to do the best we can for the students at our schools. Our community realizes the success of our students is tied to the success of our after-school programs."

Juli Kwikkel, Principal
East and West Elementary Schools
Storm Lake, Iowa

Students look to adults for models of behavior. They are hungry for guidance and mentoring. For students who lack strong parental guidance at home, after-school programs may be among the few places where young people have the chance to meet role models who take the time to get to know them. Young people who struggle academically in school could particularly benefit from having contact with other adults who take an interest in their lives.

Encourage families to support and participate in after-school learning.

Families often feel unsure about how to approach teachers and school administrators. For some families, school evokes uncomfortable memories of negative experiences. It may be a daunting prospect for parents who have had a difficult history with schools, or for immigrant families who may not speak fluent English, to approach principals and other school staff.

After-school settings can begin to bridge those divides by providing a more informal and comfortable environment for families. Simply by remaining open later, they offer an accessible entrée into a child's learning environment. They are also smaller and more personalized than schools, offering more opportunities for parent involvement.

FOCUS ON PRACTICE

After-School Programs: A Bridge Between School and Community

Tammy Condren, Principal

Marion C. Early Elementary School, Morrisville, Missouri

After-school programs are becoming a focal point of community life at Marion C. Early Elementary School. The pre-K-5 school is led by veteran principal Tammy Condren, who for the past two decades has helped develop after-school programs by working closely with parents and community members in this rural town north of Springfield, MO.

When Condren first arrived as a new principal, she looked to a local YMCA as a source of after-school activities. The YMCA, however, required a minimum number of students to participate in after-school programs, and each year it seemed her elementary school of 376 students fell one or two students short. The school changed strategy and decided it could fill the void of after-school activities for students by starting its own programs.

Surveys were sent out to parents to explore their interest in after-school activities. This helped motivate a few parents to organize and write a grant proposal to obtain funding to jumpstart programs. One of those parents became the after-school coordinator. Condren describes her local community as an important source of ongoing support and ideas for after-school programs.

The elementary school, which has a largely white student population with 70 percent of students poor enough to qualify for federal free and reduced-price lunch, has established partnerships with Ozark Food Harvest and the Salvation Army to run the state's only school-based Kids Café. Dinner is served each evening not only for students in after-school programs, but also for their parents and anyone else from the community as well.

The service is particularly welcome in a rural area where many students participating in after-school activities are at school until 6 p.m. and wait for parents to make long commutes to pick them up. Condren also worked with the Ozark Food Harvest to become a pilot site for a food assistance program at the school that provides low-income students with a backpack of healthy food on Fridays to take home to their family for the weekend.

The program also includes a "beach club," which provides after-school reading support. Students spread out towels on the floor and read with teachers in a relaxed setting. While the club is designed to nurture enjoyment of reading, it also keeps students on track academically in a state where a law requires that all students not reading within a year of their grade level be retained. Another popular activity is the PAWS program (Positive Atmosphere With Structure), which begins with a snack provided by Ozark Food Harvest and continues in the school's gym with play and time for homework help.

After-school programs at the school are fee-based, but the $5 a day fee is waived for low-income parents.

"You have to be a support system to the community," Condren says. "Here in a rural area the school is the hub of the community. We are providing for our students not just for the academics, but also for the whole person. We also support their families, who in turn support our educational program."

When after-school programs engage families, they are also more likely to have success with young people. An evaluation of the Polk Bros. Foundation's Full Service Schools Initiative in Chicago found that one of the strongest predictors of students' consistent participation in programs was how frequently their parents were involved with activities and viewed as welcome visitors. To encourage family participation, the sites hold events such as annual spring picnics, where they provide food and transportation for parents and students. The full-service schools also encourage parents to sit on oversight committees made up of school staff and representatives from community-based organizations so that parents have a voice in programming.

An evaluation of family engagement with 21st Century Community Learning Centers—a federal program that provides expanded learning opportunities for youth—found that after-school programs are particularly effective in engaging parents in after-school initiatives when they:

- Provide parents a range of counseling, support groups and referrals to social service agencies
- Offer adult education opportunities such as GED preparation and English and basic literacy classes
- Hold special "family nights" where youth and parents can enjoy cultural or recreational activities together

Principals should welcome family involvement as a means to help children and parents strengthen relationships, build trust and communication between parents and school leaders and offer families the chance to develop their own skills in a structured setting.

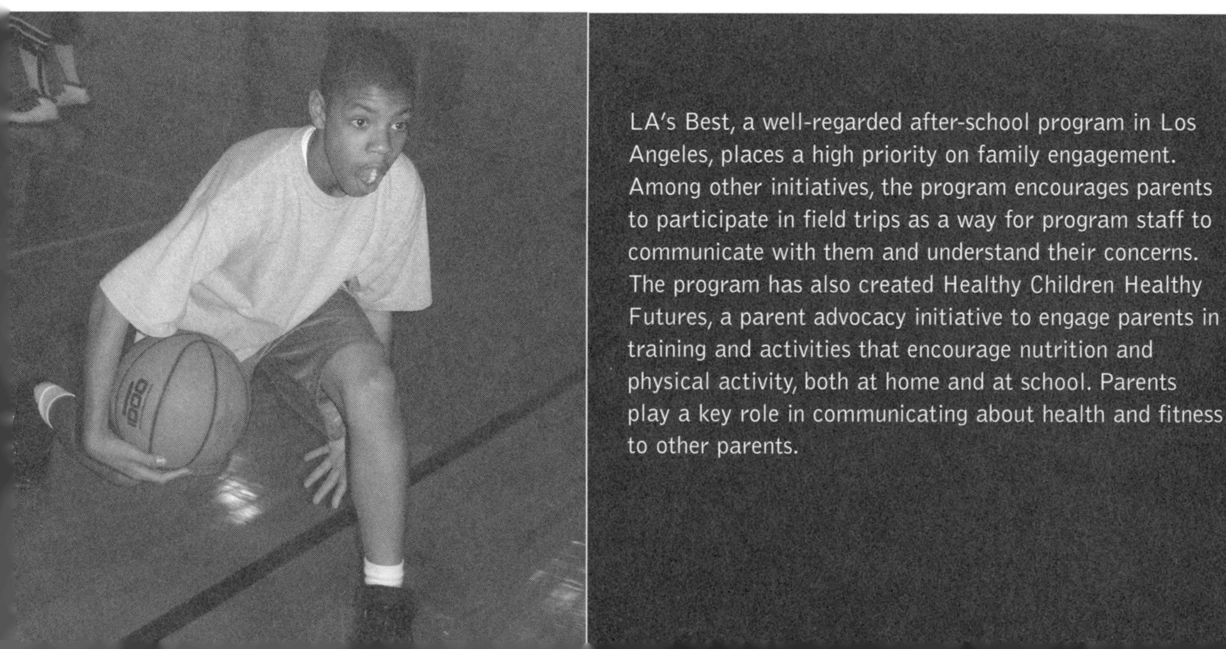

LA's Best, a well-regarded after-school program in Los Angeles, places a high priority on family engagement. Among other initiatives, the program encourages parents to participate in field trips as a way for program staff to communicate with them and understand their concerns. The program has also created Healthy Children Healthy Futures, a parent advocacy initiative to engage parents in training and activities that encourage nutrition and physical activity, both at home and at school. Parents play a key role in communicating about health and fitness to other parents.

QUESTIONS FOR FURTHER REFLECTION

Collaborate with stakeholders to create learning opportunities for students beyond the traditional school day.

- Does my leadership style facilitate collaborative work with external partners?
- Do we welcome partners into our building?
- Have we reached out to a broad range of potential community partners—government agencies, colleges/university partners, local service providers, business leaders and community groups—to create learning opportunities beyond the school day?

Facilitate development of an after-school plan that identifies and addresses needs of students and the community.

- Do we know what our students' after-school needs are?
- Do we know what the needs of the families and the broader community are?
- Have we conducted a needs assessment to determine those needs?
- Have I, as principal, helped to facilitate the development of an after-school plan?
- Has our team engaged students, parents and community partners in the planning process?
- Have we visited other after-school programs to see how they work?

Connect students with a diverse group of role models who will help ensure their success.

- Do I see the potential of after-school programs for connecting students to a broad range of positive adult role models?
- Do I look for ways to bring diverse adult role models into the building for the after-school program?
- Do I encourage adults I meet to serve as teachers, tutors and mentors?
- Does the after-school program provide the supports adults from the community need (e.g., orientation, training and ongoing feedback) to successfully work with young people?

Encourage families to support and participate in after-school learning.

- How do we encourage families to support and participate in after-school learning?
- Is the after-school program accessible to the range of families we serve?
- Are parent materials—newsletters or notes, for instance—translated into appropriate languages?
- Does the after-school program schedule events so that parents can attend?
- Does it provide the supports, e.g., childcare, transportation, parents need to be able to attend events?
- Does the program provide a full range of services to families?

PLANNING TOOL

This assessment is designed to help you and your leadership team reflect periodically on your school practice. Look back at your answers to the Questions for Further Reflection as you complete the tool. Take the assessment at the beginning, middle and end of the year to track your progress. Note things you want to change or are doing well.

Once you have mastered an item, shift your focus to other items. You may add to the assessment if you discover additional indicators you would like to track. If a question is not applicable, leave it blank. Rate each question from 1 to 4: **1** Not at all, **2** Sometimes, **3** Most of the time, **4** Always

Collaborate with stakeholders to create learning opportunities for students beyond the traditional school day.	Beginning Rating	Middle Rating	End Rating
My leadership style encourages collaborative work with external partners.			
We welcome partners into our building.			
We reach out to a broad range of community partners, including:			
government agencies			
colleges/university partners			
local service providers			
business leaders			
community groups			
Facilitate development of an after-school plan that identifies andaddresses the needs of students and the community.			
We know what our students' after-school needs are.			
We know what the needs of families and the broader community are.			
I am helping to facilitate the development of an after-school plan.			
Our team has engaged partners in the planning process, including:			
students			
parents			
community partners			
We have visited other after-school programs.			
We have a vibrant after-school plan in place.			

Connect students with a diverse group of role models who will help ensure their success.	Beginning Rating	Middle Rating	End Rating
Diverse adult role models participatein the after-school program.			
Our team encourages adults we meet to serve as after-school teachers, tutors and mentors.			
The after-school program provides supports adults need to successfully work with young people, including:			
orientation			
training			
ongoing feedback			
Encourage families to support and participate in after-school learning.			
The after-school program is accessible to the range of families we serve.			
Parent materials, such as newsletters and notes, are translated into appropriate languages.			
We provide the supports parents need to attend events, including:			
childcare			
transportation			
convenient times			
The program provides a full range of services to families.			

NOTES

FOR MORE INFORMATION

Resources From NAESP

Fagan, J. "Extended Learning for Children of Poverty." *Principal, Beyond the Bell*, Vol. 82, No. 5. May/June 2003.

National Association of Elementary School Principals. "Implementing Effective After-School Programs." *Here's How*, Vol. 7. No. 3. March 1999.

On the Web

Afterschool Matters (www.fdncenter.org/grantmaker/bowne/journal.html), a Robert Bowne Foundation journal, provides informative articles from both practitioners and researchers on current after-school issues.

Coalition for Community Schools (www.communityschools.org) works to improve education and help students learn and grow while supporting and strengthening their families and communities. It provides toolkits, resources and a newsletter on ways to build school-community partnerships around school-day and after-school.

The Family Involvement Network of Educators (www.gse.harvard.edu/hfrp/projects/fine.html) is a national network of more than 5,000 people who are interested in promoting strong partnerships among children's educators, their families and their communities, including after-school programs. Resources on the FINE Web site include a Web-based guide to family-involvement resources for after-school.

Innovation Center for Community and Youth Development (www.theinnovationcenter.org) is a hub of innovative practices for continuous collaboration among schools, after-school programs and the community.

Learning Point Associates (www.learningpt.org) provides three key online tools to help principals support after-school: Beyond the Bell (www.beyondthebell.org), Beyond the Bell Principal's Guide (www.beyondthebell.org/page_principalguide.php) and Strengthening Connections Between Schools and After-School Programs (www.learningpt.org/page.php?pageID=166).

National Center for Family and Community Connections with Schools (www.sedl.org/connections/about.html) offers research-based information and resources to effectively connect schools, families and communities. The center reviews emerging findings and research to develop an online database, annual conferences and reports to help advance procedural knowledge and provides training and networking across the Regional Educational Laboratories system to link research findings to practice.

From the Research

Afterschool Alliance. "Afterschool Programs Strengthen Communities." *Afterschool Alert Issue Brief*, No. 18. January 2004.

Foundations, Inc. *Homework Zone Kit.* Moorestown, NJ: Foundations, Inc., undated.

Harris, E. and Wimer, C. "Engaging With Families in Out-of-School Time Learning." *Out-of-School Time Evaluation Snapshot*, No. 4. Cambridge, MA: Harvard Family Research Project, April 2004.

Iowa Afterschool Alliance. *A Guide for Afterschool Community Forums.* Des Moines, IA: 2005.

Kaplan, C. *Opening Doors for Boston's Children: Lessons Learned in Expanding School-Based After-School Programs.* Boston, MA: Boston's After-School for All Partnership, October 2004.

Peterson, T. "Engaging and Enriching Afterschool Programs Through Statewide and Local Partnerships: Giving Children and Youth the Opportunities and Connections To Keep Them on Track." Remarks for North Carolina Center for Afterschool Programs Regional Meetings in Asheville and Winston-Salem, NC. Charleston, SC: Afterschool and Community Learning Network, November 2003.

Polman, J., et al. "Youth Programs in the Community Context." *Afterschool Matters*, No. 3. New York, NY: Spring 2004.

Weiss, A. R. and Brigham, R. A. *The Family Participation in After-School Study.* Boston, MA: Institute for Responsive Education, 2003.

Whalen, S. P. *Report of the Evaluation of the Polk Bros. Foundation Full Service School Initiative.* Chicago, IL: University of Chicago, April 2002.

3

Infrastructure

Collaborate with program directors to manage resources that support the full learning day.

Seamless coordination between school and after-school programs enables programs to manage resources efficiently and to operate smoothly.

Principals are not expected to be the primary managers of after-school programs. School leaders already have a full load of responsibilities to balance. Instead, effective principals delegate responsibilities and work in tandem with program directors. Principals help build support for after-school funding, coordinate schedules and use of facilities, ensure a safe environment for students and help shape the content of after-school activities. Principals and program directors draw upon each other's strengths and recognize that they must have a strong relationship to leverage resources to support and sustain quality after-school initiatives.

Creating this collaborative approach is challenging. School and after-school environments often have their own norms and institutional cultures. Principals must be clear about roles, expectations and accountability when partnering with community-based organizations, foundations and other social service agencies that often manage after-school programs at school or at off-site locations.

Principals who collaborate with program directors to manage resources that support the full learning day:

- Hold programs accountable to expectations jointly developed with the program director
- Ensure that after-school programs are well managed and employ sound fiscal practices
- Create formal and informal communication strategies between the principal and the program director and the school and after-school staff members
- Develop a positive culture between school and after-school staff members and mediate concerns when they arise
- Provide appropriate resources when the program is implemented (including facilities, security, custodial services, storage, cafeterias, secretarial support, technology, supplies and telephones)

Hold programs accountable to expectations jointly developed with the program director.

Principals who support extended learning opportunities make sure after-school programs meet high standards across a range of areas. They work collaboratively with program directors to establish a framework that guides this work. This framework helps set mutual goals, rationales for standards and ways to assess whether programs are being effectively implemented.

"Through my experiences, I have learned that principals have to be involved in after-school programs to make them run smoothly. It's all connected."

Kathy Corley, Principal
Sara Harp Minter Elementary
Fayettesville, Georgia

School leaders pay attention to how programs are meeting established goals and expectations, in part by visiting after-school activities and meeting with program directors for reflective discussions. This attentiveness helps keep school and after-school leaders focused on consistent improvement and sends a signal about the value of the after-school program to the school.

Research points to the importance of quality staffing in establishing strong after-school programs. Principals should help after-school leaders identify the critical factors important in hiring staff, should invite teachers into after-school programs and should include after-school staff in professional development.

After-school settings must be safe. Safety is often the first thing parents are looking for in after-school programs, because young people risk getting involved with harmful behaviors in the hours after the school day ends. Principals and program directors should develop a system for monitoring safety together and promptly address students' and parents' concerns about the quality of the facility, how accessible the building is to unidentified visitors and ways security can be improved.

Ensure that after-school programs are well managed and employ sound fiscal practices.

The most ingenious ideas and ambitious plans for after-school will never be realized without effective management and financial stability. How after-school programs are managed will depend on the particulars of the program.

When after-school initiatives are based in schools, principals have a more direct responsibility for how the programs are operated and funded. The management and financial structure of programs operated by an outside community organization, foundation or social service provider may be different, however. In these cases, even if the program is not housed in a school, principals and program directors should work together to ensure that programs are led effectively and that budgets are balanced.

Principals who help establish efficient management practices and sound fiscal policies:

- Include program directors in budget development and monitoring
- Hold management review meetings throughout the year to clarify expectations and discuss leadership challenges
- Include after-school in auditing assessments of the school's finances

"Principals need to know how to work in out-of-school time and how to shift to a more collaborative leadership style. It's about shared leadership and responsibility. It takes a different kind of leader to make that happen."

Martin Blank
Coalition for Community Schools

The National Institute on Out-of-School Time maintains a clearinghouse on after-school education, training and compensation. This online tool contains valuable resources for principals and program directors.
www.niost.org/clearinghouse/index.html

Create formal and informal communication strategies between the principal and the program director and school and after-school staff members.

Principals and program directors recognize that ongoing dialogue is crucial to supporting the development of exemplary after-school programs.

Communication between principals and program directors must be clear, consistent and grounded in a common understanding about what the goals are for after-school learning.

By regularly checking in with program directors, principals show they are engaged and accessible. This helps create a sense of camaraderie between principals and program directors that can go a long way toward building trust and respect. School leaders also deepen their understanding of how after-school settings operate, including what specific challenges directors encounter, when they spend time getting to know programs firsthand.

Principals should also encourage teachers to help in after-school programs. After-school staff and teachers have a natural, shared interest in students' learning and development that can be deepened by opportunities to work together more frequently. These collaborations also help students see that teachers can be trusted as adults who have a genuine interest in them beyond the classroom.

Teachers who may have an interest in offering special classes such as arts or drama that they may not have time for during the school day are prime candidates for work with after-school programs. Principals might provide financial incentives to teachers who take on significant roles in after-school.

"We are educational experts and should be involved in after-school programs, but we don't necessarily need to be managing programs."

Jill Flanders, Principal
Plains Elementary School
South Hadley, Massachusetts

Principals may consider having the program director attend staff meetings at the school. This provides program directors with the opportunity to report on progress and challenges, as well as to explore ways school and after-school staff can more effectively work in coordination. If the after-school coordinator is part-time, he or she may also be invited to work in school as a resource teacher or curriculum support staff member during the day.

Some principals have found it helpful to have the program director's office located in the school's central office. This physical proximity can help improve communication and also sends a powerful message that after-school is an integral part of the school's mission. Something as simple as having a designated mailbox in school for the program director can also break down some of the barriers between school and after-school communities.

"There must be solid communication between who is running the after-school program and the school. Things regularly happen in after-school programs that significantly impact the school day and principal. Somebody needs to be able to deal with those issues as they arise."

Claudia Weisburd, Foundations, Inc.

Develop a positive culture between school and after-school staff members and mediate concerns when they arise.

Principals who take steps to promote a culture of mutual respect between school and after-school staff:

- Share classrooms, libraries and other school facilities with after-school programs
- Create opportunities for teachers to participate in after-school activities and find ways to incorporate after-school staff into the school day
- Act as diplomats when turf issues undermine a collaborative approach to helping students

Unfortunately, in too many cases school and after-school staff members are isolated from one another and unaware of what is taking place in each other's learning communities. After-school professionals often feel left out, underappreciated and disconnected from the school culture. Teachers who leave when the school day ends sometimes assume that after-school programs have little relevance to their work.

Principals have the potential to create a new paradigm by encouraging opportunities for school and after-school staff to work together on projects that link school and after-school learning. If there is a shared curriculum calendar, for example, school and after-school staff may work on complementary projects. Principals set a tone for good relations and seek common ground where teachers and after-school staff can learn from one another. Creating a smooth working relationship between school staff and after-school staff can help ensure quality programming and operations.

When tensions over use of space, program scheduling and other matters arise, principals look for practical solutions and compromises that respect the perspectives of both school and after-school staff. Principals remind everyone that the ultimate goal is helping students have meaningful learning experiences—wherever they take place.

Provide appropriate resources when the program is implemented (including facilities, security, custodial services, storage, cafeterias, secretarial support, technology, supplies and telephones).

Some of the most contentious issues between school and after-school staffs center on facilities and equipment. The After-School Corporation, which operates a system of school-based after-school programs in New York City, found that some programs lacked access to facilities such as libraries, computer labs and office space. Teachers were often hesitant to share classroom space because they feared supplies would be stolen or rooms would not be clean at the end of the evening. After-school staff in these sites helped solve these problems by using checklists posted outside the classroom to help monitor classroom conditions, hosting breakfasts and other special events to foster teachers' support for after-school programs and offering books and art supplies to classroom teachers in appreciation for their cooperation.

Principals and program directors who help ensure after-school programs have access to agreed-upon resources:

- Map out what resources will be needed on an ongoing basis
- Meet annually to discuss gaps in resources and budgetary issues that nee to be addressed
- Seek resources through grants that cover both in-school and out-of-school time

Transportation Ideas for Your School

Transportation poses a challenge for many after-school programs. The challenge is especially acute in rural areas, where students are often dependent on busing to get to school.

- Adjust the bus departure times from your school to leave when after-school programs are finished
- Share a "late bus" or an "activities bus" with other school or non-school activities
- Partner with community organizations to provide activities in satellite locations in the neighborhoods where your participants live

Reprinted from *Beyond the Bell: A Principal's Guide to Effective Afterschool Programs* with permission from Learning Points Associates.

FOCUS ON PRACTICE

Enlisting Help to Achieve Success

Janette Hewitt, Principal
George Washington Elementary School, Lancaster, Pennsylvania

Janette Hewitt knew she couldn't implement an after-school program that met the needs of children, families and the community at George Washington Elementary School on her own.

Hewitt, 13-year principal of the K-5 school, credits the success of extended learning opportunities at the school with the hard work of community school coordinator Annette Rosa-Pabon. "I've known for years that we weren't able to meet the many needs of our boys, girls and families," says Hewitt. "It's only been in the last three years—with Annette working with the school—that we've been able to offer the kinds of supports that our students and families need."

George Washington is a community school with a mission and vision that supports the academic, social and emotional needs of students, families and the community. As community school coordinator, Rosa-Pabon is responsible for creating and supporting programs that help children and families succeed—including an after-school program that involves 178 of the school's 620 students.

An important key to the program's success has been Hewitt's and Rosa-Pabon's collaborative leadership. Hewitt says open communication and transparency are essential to making a principal-coordinator partnership work. Hewitt and Rosa-Pabon operate on a shared calendar and meet at least once a week to discuss program successes and challenges. The pair draws from their respective experiences in education and social services to overcome barriers and implement a program that extends the school's vision and expectations.

Hewitt knew that if she was going to get a coordinator on board who "got" what the school was trying to accomplish, she would have to be involved in the selection process. She looked for someone with a strong background in social services, who understood the community the school was trying to serve and the way in which after-school programs could best serve that population. At George Washington, where 71 percent of students are Latino, it was important that the coordinator speak Spanish and that she or he understood the challenges of the students, 90 percent of whom qualify for free or reduced-price lunch.

Hewitt and Rosa-Pabon have started to see results from their work. In 2003-04, the school for the first time made adequate yearly progress under the federal No Child Left Behind Act in math, reading and attendance. In 2004-05 the school maintained its rate of growth in all areas. Their inclusive leadership style has encouraged others to get involved with the program. Nearly all of the tutors in the extended day program are teachers from the school, and parents have started coming in during and after school, looking for ways to help.

While Hewitt stresses that starting an after-school program is hard work and requires attention, she notes that it can be done when there is someone on board who is ready and able to help. "It's worth it," she says. "It's changed the way I lead in this community and this school."

Responsibility Checklist for the Principal and After-School Program Coordinator

Directions: The principal and after-school program coordinator should complete this checklist together. Review the tasks in column 1. Add any additional tasks that may be needed. Then, for each task in column 1, indicate who will be responsible—the principal or program coordinator—or whether it will be a shared responsibility. If a responsibility will be shared, decide how it will be shared.

Task	Responsibility of Principal	Responsibility of After-School Coordinator	Shared Responsibility (Indicate How)
Secure space for after-school activities.			
Inform classroom teachers that their classrooms will be used.			
Provide supplies and materials for after-school programs.			
Handle discipline issues that arise in after-school programs.			
Communicate with parents about the content of after-school programs.			
Recruit students for after-school programs.			
Decide which activities will be offered.			

Task	Responsibility of Principal	Responsibility of After-School Coordinator	Shared Responsibility (Indicate How)
Involve school staff in curriculum and activity development.			
Hire and supervise after-school program staff.			
Register participants for after-school programs.			
Communicate with classroom teachers about homework.			
Provide professional development for after-school staff members.			
Manage the after-school budget.			
Collect fees from students and raise program funds.			
Develop an evaluation framework; collect and analyze data; share evaluation results.			
Share information about the program with the community and general public.			

Adapted from *Beyond the Bell: A Principal's Guide to Effective Afterschool Programs,* Learning Point Associates, 2005, pp. 26-27.

Job Description for After-School Program Coordinator

Use the outline below to craft a job description for this position.

DEFINITION

An individual who is recruited, selected and employed by either the school district or a community-based agency to oversee the programs, activities and collaborative process in a comprehensive after-school program.

TITLE (What will this person be called?)

Program Manager; After-School Coordinator; Program Director

QUALIFICATIONS

What educational background should this person have? Does the person need to be a certified administrator? How many years of work experience should the person have? Does it matter where that work experience has been? In determining qualifications, keep in mind the responsibilities this person will have. The more responsibilities assigned to the job, the more experience and education you may want to require.

REPORTS TO/SUPERVISES

To whom does this position report? Who will evaluate this person? How often? Which positions, if any, are supervised by this person?

RESPONSIBILITIES (Select the ones that apply to the position.)

- Coordinates the development and implementation of the after-school program.
- Hires, trains and supervises staff; facilitates professional development of staff.
- Communicates with parents and students about the after-school program.
- Establishes and maintains communication with members of the school staff about student needs and other relevant aspects of the after-school program.
- Implements applicable district, agency and grant policies and regulations.
- Develops and administers the after-school budget.
- Provides oral and written reports to the public and the school system.
- Develops and facilitates partnerships with appropriate public and private agencies that provide services to the students and families.
- Develops procedures and policies for operation of the after-school program.
- Works with the principal and an advisory board to develop and implement a sustainability plan for the after-school program.
- Prepares grant proposals and other requests for supplemental funding.
- Oversees evaluation activities; analyzes and applies information from program evaluations.
- Participates on local and state committees related to after-school programs.
- Maintains records needed for program administration.

SPECIAL REQUIREMENTS

Does the person require a car? Will the person have to travel frequently? Does the person need to speak any languages other than English? Are there any aspects of the job that require any special skills? Does this person need to submit to a background check or drug testing?

Adapted from *Beyond the Bell: A Principal's Guide to Effective Afterschool Programs,* Learning Point Associates, 2005, pp. 26-27.

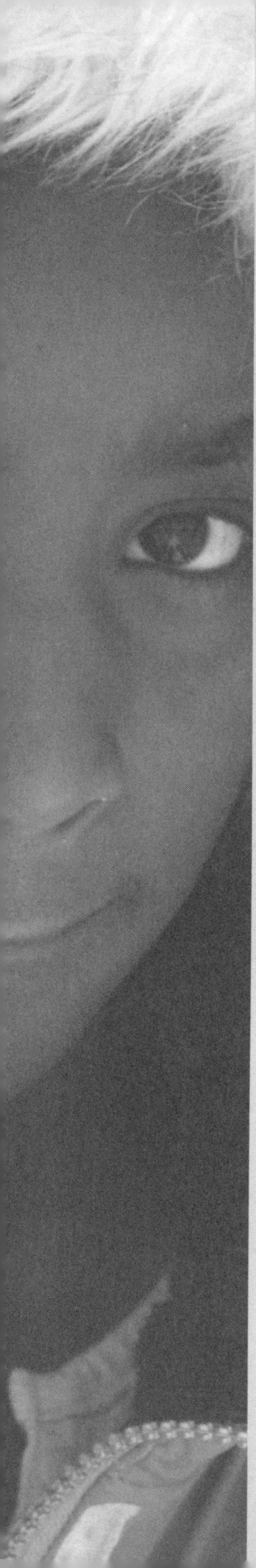

FOCUS ON PRACTICE

Creating an After-School Program Infrastructure That Puts Students' Needs First

Haydee Alvarez, Principal
Horace Greeley Elementary School, Chicago, Illinois

"Finally, something for me!" exclaimed a student after learning about the mural-painting class in Horace Greeley Elementary's after-school program.

From Principal Haydee Alvarez's perspective, offering a rich menu of program choices that meets students' diverse needs is one of the keys to a successful after-school program.

Alvarez's school, a K-8 elementary, situated in the East Lakeview community near Wrigley Field, serves a high concentration of Latino students—they make up almost 70 percent of Greeley's 550 students—and recent immigrants from Russia and Eastern Europe. Students speak a variety of languages at home.

The primary challenge Alvarez faced as she planned the after-school program in collaboration with the school's after-school partners was how to provide students with extra help, while at the same time enabling them to participate in enrichment activities such as Mexican folkloric dance, drama and band.

Greeley's after-school partners—After-School Counts, a Chicago Public Schools sponsored program that provides remedial reading and math classes; After-School All-Stars, also a CPS sponsored program that offers enrichment activities for students in grades 4-8; and Urban Gateways, an arts program and the school's 21st Century Community Learning Centers partner—worked with Alvarez to schedule program activities so that students would be able to receive academic assistance *and* paint murals, if that activity interested them.

Alvarez explains her solution to the challenge: "We offer the enrichment reading and math/science clubs on the same day and times as the remedial reading and math classes—Monday, Tuesday and Thursday. All other enrichment activities are offered on Wednesdays and Fridays in order to allow students who need remediation to participate. In addition, we offer band and chorus in the morning to accommodate bus students."

Greeley also has a high poverty rate—over 92 percent of students are eligible for free or reduced-priced lunch—and many parents work long hours. Alvarez works closely with two part-time after-school coordinators and her after-school partners, especially Urban Gateways, to plan a program infrastructure that meets the needs of working families. One way Greeley meets those needs is through Wolf-Trap—an early morning literacy and fine arts program for kindergarten to 3rd grade students.

By all accounts, Alvarez and her partners' efforts are paying off: Students and families love the after-school program.

QUESTIONS FOR FURTHER REFLECTION

Hold programs accountable to expectations jointly developed with the program director.

- Do we (I, as principal, and the program director) have shared expectations for the program?
- Have we established a framework for assessing how well we are meeting these expectations?
- Do I, or members of my team, meet regularly with the program director to discuss program goals and expectations?

Ensure that after-school programs are well managed and employ sound fiscal practices.

- For school-based programs, are there clear lines of authority between the principal and the program director?
- Are program directors included in budget development and monitoring processes?
- Are management concerns addressed when they arise?
- Are management review meetings held regularly?

Create formal and informal communication strategies between the principal and the program director and school and after-school staff members.

- Do I communicate frequently with the program director?
- Do I copy the program director on relevant school communications?
- Is the program director welcome to attend school staff meetings?
- Do I encourage the program director to share after-school news with school staff?
- Do I drop by the after-school program regularly?
- Is the program director's office near mine?
- Am I accessible to her/him?

Develop a positive culture between school and after-school staff members and mediate concerns when they arise.

- Are school staff members welcome to participate in after-school activities?
- Do I encourage school staff members to reach out to after-school staff and vice versa?
- Do I serve as mediator when differences between school and after-school staff members arise?
- Am I working with the program director to create a positive school culture that extends beyond the regular school day?

Provide appropriate resources when the program is implemented.

- Have we (the program director and I, along with the school leadership team) mapped out what resources will be shared?
- Do we meet annually to discuss gaps in resources?
- Do members of both staffs (school and after-school) have a clear understanding of what resources are shared, how and why?
- Do we have devices in place—such as checklists—that help staff members monitor shared resources?
- Does the school have the capacity to provide necessary resources?
- Have we looked for funding to support both school and after-school activities?

PLANNING TOOL

This assessment is designed to help you and your leadership team reflect periodically on your school practice. Look back at your answers to the Questions for Further Reflection as you complete the tool. Take the assessment at the beginning, middle and end of the year to track your progress. Note things you want to change or are doing well.

Once you have mastered an item, shift your focus to other items. You may add to the assessment if you discover additional indicators you would like to track. If a question is not applicable, leave it blank. Rate each question from 1 to 4: **1** Not at all, **2** Sometimes, **3** Most of the time, **4** Always

Hold programs accountable to expectations jointly developed with the program director.	Beginning Rating	Middle Rating	End Rating
The program director and I have shared expectations for the program.			
The program director and I have a framework for assessing how well we are meeting expectations.			
I meet regularly with the program director to discuss goals and expectations.			
Ensure that after-school programs are well managed and employ sound fiscal practices.			
There are clear lines of authority between the program director and me.			
If school-based, the program director is included in budget development and monitoring processes.			
Management review meetings are held regularly.			
Management concerns are addressed immediately.			

Create formal and informal communication strategies between the principal and the program director and the school and after-school staff members.	Beginning Rating	Middle Rating	End Rating
I am accessible to the program director.			
I copy the program director on school communications.			
The program director attends school staff meetings.			
The program director shares after-school news with school staff members.			
I encourage teachers and after-school staff members to meet.			
I drop by the after-school program frequently.			
Develop a positive culture between school and after-school staff members and mediate concerns when they arise.			
I communicate the message that both in-school and after-school staff members are valued members of our school team.			
School staff members are welcome to participate in after-school activities and vice versa.			
I serve as a neutral mediator when concerns arise between school and after-school staff members.			
I work with the program director to build a positive culture between school and after-school staff members.			
Provide appropriate resources when the program is implemented.			
The program director and I have a clear understanding of what resources the school will provide.			
School and after-school staffs understand which resources are shared, how they are shared and why they are shared.			
We have checklists that help staff monitor shared resources.			
The program director and I meet to discuss gaps in resources and ways of filling those gaps.			
We look for funding to support school and after-school activities.			

FOR MORE INFORMATION

Resources From NAESP

Lauer, R. "After-School Programs: Everybody's Doing It." *Principal, Beyond the Bell*, Vol. 82, No. 5. May/June 2003.

Rinehart, J. "A Principal's Fulfilled Vision." *Principal, Beyond the Bell*, Vol. 82, No. 5. May/June 2003.

On the Web

The After-School Corporation (www.tascorp.org) provides training, technical assistance, toolkits and resources to leaders running after-school programs.

Experience Corps (www.experiencecorps.org) provides research on ways principals can engage community and older adults in supporting student achievement through tutoring and mentoring.

Fight Crime: Invest in Kids (www.fightcrime.org) gives principals and after-school providers information on ways to create a safe and secure after-school environment for students.

School-Age Notes (www.afterschoolcatalog.com) provides a catalog of resources to help principals and program directors run and support an effective after-school program.

Southwest Educational Development Laboratory (www.sedl.org/pubs/fam95/) resource guide for after-school provides school leaders management, communication and programming steps necessary to support after-school programs.

From the Research

Bagby, J. H. *A Resource Guide for Planning and Operating After-School Programs* (2nd Ed.). Austin, TX: Southwest Educational Development Laboratory, 2004.

The Finance Project. "Creating Dedicated Local Revenue Sources for Out-of-School Time Initiatives." *Strategy Brief*, Vol. 1. September 1999.

The Finance Project. "Finding Resources to Support Rural Out-of-School Time Initiatives." *Strategy Brief*, Vol. 4. No. 1. February 2003.

Learning Point Associates. *Beyond the Bell: A Principal's Guide to Effective Afterschool Programs*. Chicago, IL: 2005.

National Institute on Out-of-School Time and the Academy for Educational Development Center for Youth Development and Policy Research. *Strategic Plan: Building a Skilled and Stable Out-of-School Time Workforce*. Wellesley, MA: 2003.

Policy Studies Associates. "After-School Homework Help." *A TASC Brief*. Washington, DC: May 2001.

Wimer, C., Post, M. and Little, P. "Leveraging Resources To Promote Positive School-CBO Relationships." *Afterschool Matters*, No. 3. Spring 2004.

4

Quality Content

Support linkages, connections and relationships between the school day and after-school learning that ensure program content meets community, school and student needs.

After-school programs are not islands adrift from the broader goals of schools and communities. In too many cases, however, an invisible wall divides the school day from after-school.

By creating a seamless learning day, principals and after-school leaders create a more coherent experience for young people. They help students make deeper connections with adults both inside and out of school and offer young people added resources that can support them academically and socially.

The pressure of academic standards and assessments is a reality in schools today. From superintendents to classroom teachers, educators' attention is centered on linking curriculum frameworks to rigorous standards that can be measured by grade level assessments. State accountability exams and No Child Left Behind requirements have placed additional responsibilities on schools to improve the academic performance of all students, regardless of race, ethnicity, special needs and income level.

While after-school programs are not directly accountable for student achievement, they do have the potential to support and enrich standards-based learning. The unique culture of after-school programs allows for creative teaching strategies, multi-age learning groups and extended blocks of learning time. Arts projects and practical science activities enhance classroom-based learning.

After-school programs can also expand learning by focusing on concepts and activities not covered in state standards during the school day. They provide an ideal setting to explore physical health and wellness, community service activities and mentoring programs. And they provide opportunities for student enrichment by enabling students to explore special interests in greater depth.

Students, teachers, parents and other community members all have a role in shaping the content of quality after-school programs. Active engagement encourages an attitude of personal ownership and investment and helps ensure the activities have relevance in the eyes of the community.

While specific activities in after-school programs will reflect the particular needs of schools and communities, quality programs generally offer a mix of tutoring, homework help, enrichment and recreational and cultural activities.

Principals who support linkages, connections and relationships between the school day and after-school learning that ensure program content meets community, school and students needs:

- Ensure that the school's learning and core academic standards are connected to activities in after-school programs
- Offer learning opportunities in after-school that are different from, but connected to, those in the school day
- Provide a continuum of services and supports for students (including homework assistance, enrichment, tutoring, extra-curricular clubs, service and civic development opportunities, mentoring, arts, technology, foreign language and healthy snacks)
- Connect professional development opportunities for after-school and school day staff members to ensure consistency in standards of teaching and learning and to encourage relationship-building among staff members

"Our after-school staff members get the same professional development as school day staff."

Margaret Scott, Principal Fairview Elementary Fairfax Station, Virginia

Ensure that the school's learning and core academic standards are connected to activities in after-school programs.

After-school settings approach learning and youth development in creative ways that do not simply mirror what happens during the school day. However, activities should be informed by the school's academic standards and reinforce key learning concepts when appropriate.

Principals can help promote this connection by sharing academic standards for each grade level with program directors and staff members. In turn, they may encourage program directors to share their program goals for the year with school staff. This kind of transparency helps everyone think more specifically about opportunities to reinforce skills that students are expected to learn.

Inviting program directors to sit in on academic planning meetings helps foster an expanded community of teaching and learning and encourages after-school staff and principals to strategize together about how after-school enrichment can be better tailored to meet students' needs. Simply sharing a list of after-school participants with classroom teachers will let them know which students are available for additional support when the school day ends.

Teachers should participate in after-school planning and programs as much as possible. They might act as curriculum consultants for after-school programs or provide mentoring or tutoring services. Teachers involved in after-school programming can also serve as after-school ambassadors to school staff. They become important connectors between the school and after-school communities.

There are many ways to consider linking a school's academic curriculum with after-school. If a standard for social studies, for example, requires knowledge of the geography of the United States, an after-school arts program could have children work together to draw a large map with colored chalk on a blacktop pavement. When science standards focus on recycling, the after-school program might host a recyclable material art fair, reinforcing academic concepts in an engaging way. Learning concepts can also be incorporated into sports, board games and musical activities.

Offering students opportunities to read for pleasure through book clubs, library visits or simple quiet times can enhance literacy by engendering a love for reading and expanding children's vocabularies. Such opportunities are particularly important for many adolescents who seldom read outside of class.

The Children's Aid Society has developed after-school programs at community schools throughout New York City that integrate children's literature with fun activities such as creative writing and visual and dramatic arts. The activities, which support the New York state standards in English language arts, are developed jointly with the schools they serve and use programs known as KidzLit (www.devstu.org/afterschool) and Foundations (www.foundationsinc.org). They are designed to help children improve literacy skills and foster broader social skills.

Offer learning opportunities in after-school that are different from, but connected to, those in the school day.

Principals recognize that after-school has the potential to get students excited about learning in settings that provide creative approaches for engaging young people.

After-school programs are particularly well suited to respond to students with different learning styles and to young people who are not succeeding in traditional school settings.

The concept of multiple intelligences, developed by Howard Gardner of Harvard University, teaches educators that young people possess a range of abilities. These intelligences include: linguistic, logical-mathematical, spatial, body-kinesthetic, musical, interpersonal, intrapersonal and naturalist. Gardner argues that schools focus most of their attention on linguistic and logical-mathematical intelligence at the expense of other abilities.

After-school settings have the potential to address multiple learning styles that may get lost amid tightly scripted curriculum plans in the classroom. A student who has trouble grasping math concepts in a textbook, for example, may excel in an after-school setting where he or she can see how math is used in everyday life.

"We try to develop activities that will keep all students—even older students—engaged. It's what we do with the program that helps keep kids there."

Mary Grant, Principal
Takoma Educational Center
Washington, D.C.

The Boys & Girls Clubs of King County, Washington, for example, has a Lego Lab as part of its after-school program. The lab uses project-based learning in science and math to help teach children about simple machines, gear systems and power-transfer systems.

A growing number of middle and high schools are starting after-school "slam" poetry clubs that give students a chance to express themselves creatively and improve writing skills. English teachers often start these clubs at the urging of students and are also integrating slam into their classes as a way to spark interest in literary expression.

Flipping the Script, a curriculum designed by the San Francisco-based nonprofit Just Think, motivates students to become critical consumers of media images and messages. The interdisciplinary curriculum, which includes subject areas such as language arts, social studies and mathematics, is often used in after-school settings. It includes a 30-page guidebook with age-appropriate lesson plans that are tied to academic content standards. The project also helps students learn how to showcase their own media projects at school fairs, community exhibitions, film festivals and other venues.

Provide a continuum of services and supports for students (including homework assistance, enrichment, tutoring, extra-curricular clubs, service and civic development opportunities, mentoring, arts, technology, foreign language and healthy snacks).

The most dynamic after-school settings offer students a rich mosaic of programs that help young people develop new skills, address areas of academic weakness and provide enrichment opportunities that enhance learning. This means that after-school programs should have broad appeal for different types of learners and students with varied interests.

One of the most important ways after-school programs can help young people learn is by giving them a strong sense of themselves as individuals and learners. Just as schools are finding that personalized attention helps young people feel more confident about their own abilities, after-school programs can empower children by helping develop their individual identities. One way of accomplishing this is by providing a space for each child to call his or her own. At the Sara Harp Minter Elementary School in Fayettesville, Georgia, each child has a tub to store materials.

After-school programs can expand their offerings by forging partnerships with local museums and other cultural institutions to provide opportunities for students to make connections with professional artists, musicians and writers. Expanding cultural competency is particularly important for students who come from low-income families and may have less exposure to the arts than middle-class children. Research shows that engagement with the arts helps students improve analytical and spatial skills, as well as motivates students to become more serious about other subjects. Inviting parents to concerts, dance recitals and other after-school cultural events can help engage adults in the school community and deepen connections between young people and their parents.

Principals recognize that after-school tutoring can provide additional time and more personalized attention for students who need support that may not be available during the regular school day. This extra help will be most beneficial to students when teachers themselves are actively involved in after-school tutoring and have consistent communication with after-school staff to make sure specific needs of individual students are being addressed.

Homework assistance is another after-school service many parents and students value. Working parents often have little time to help their children with assignments. Students fall behind when homework is incomplete. Many successful after-school programs incorporate homework help into the beginning hour of programs to help students get a head start on work.

"School leaders should think about activities they want students to pursue at home, then realize that many students don't have the opportunity to pursue those activities at home and think about how they can be provided in the after-school program."

David Poer, Principal
Williamstown Elementary School
Williamstown, Kentucky

After-school clubs can also be an enjoyable way of both supporting students' personal interests and helping them improve in specific academic areas. A national distinguished principal in Jonesboro, Arkansas, created the after-school Guys' Comic Book Club when he realized many male students in his school were falling behind in reading. He enlisted a reading teacher to sponsor the club, and for nine weeks the students read comic books together. All of the students not only improved their reading ability, but also had enjoyable experiences with a subject that had been a source of frustration for them.

"School-day teaching usually follows a direct instructional model. We all know there are other ways for children to learn. In my opinion, there are better ways for children to learn. After-school is an informal, enriching, self-discovery or experiential model, which often works better for students."

Donna Erwin, Principal
Four Georgians Elementary
Helena, Montana

Foreign language enrichment is also an area where after-school programs can stand out. As a growing number of school districts grapple with the opportunities and challenges posed by the influx of new immigrants, after-school programs can foster cultural and linguistic exchanges that help newcomers feel more welcome and give students a greater appreciation for multiculturalism. This kind of cross-cultural exchange can be particularly useful in formerly homogenous rural and suburban communities where rapid demographic changes are often accompanied by tensions and misunderstanding. Native Spanish-speaking students, for example, can help teach their language and culture by sharing ethnic food and music with their English-speaking classmates, who in turn share their own language and traditions. Inviting parents to participate in these cultural exchanges can further deepen connections between a school and community.

Connect professional development opportunities for after-school and school-day staff members to ensure consistency in standards of teaching and learning and to encourage relationship-building among staff members.

Successful principals know that the professional capacity of after-school staff members, and the degree to which they are embraced as equal partners by a school, directly impacts the experiences students will have when the school day ends.

To this end, professional development for classroom teachers should, when possible, include program directors and staff members. Collaborative professional development should address:

- Common skill sets that both teachers and after-school staff members need to help students academically, socially and emotionally
- Lessons and activities that teachers and after-school staff members can develop and implement together
- Challenges and problem areas in integrating school and after-school learning

FOCUS ON PRACTICE

Making After-School Work: A "Seamless Approach"

Yvonne Chan, Principal
Vaughn Next Century Learning Center, San Fernando, California

At Vaughn Next Century Learning Center, a pre-K-8 charter school in one of the poorest sections of Los Angeles County, after-school programs are a centerpiece of Principal Yvonne Chan's strategy to help students become better prepared for school and life.

When Chan arrived in 1990, she inherited a failing school and a patchwork of child-care activities. A comprehensive after-school program did not exist. Handpicked earlier in her career by former Los Angeles Mayor Tom Bradley to be the first principal to adopt LA's Best—now a nationally recognized after-school initiative—Chan needed little convincing about the potential benefits of after-school programs.

All of her 1,800 students are poor enough to qualify for free or reduced-price meals. Most are first-generation immigrants from Mexico, Guatemala and other Central American countries who speak Spanish at home. Parents worry about gang violence, drug use and other lures of inner-city street life that make the hours after school a dangerous time.

Chan first began developing a diverse array of after-school offerings by inviting LA's Best into the school to provide after-school enrichment. She addressed high turnover rates among after-school paraprofessionals by reaching out to community members to cultivate her own cadre of reliable after-school staff. Two classroom teachers from every grade were assigned to work in after-school programs by developing lessons and monitoring students' academic progress.

Today, 460 students participate in academic, cultural and recreational after-school programs at Vaughn. Activities include a neighborhood beautification club sponsored by Bank of America; a Nutrition Network healthy cooking class sponsored by the state's department of health; homework assistance and tutoring; a drama and performing arts club; lessons in multicultural appreciation; a basketball league; and a Cub Scouts group that helps students build civic awareness.

"It's a seamless approach," Chan says. "Our school day goes from 7 a.m. to 6 p.m., and you can't even tell who is working in school or in after-school. There is no dividing line between school and after-school. That's how we make it work."

Because the school houses pre-K through 8th grade, Chan takes advantage of this wide age range in after-school activities. In the Nutrition Network, for example, older students often prepare healthy meals and serve them to younger students. Parents are invited in to taste the food and learn about obesity, diabetes, asthma and other health issues that are common problems among low-income, urban communities.

"We have a tight organizational plan for after-school that is just as tight as that of the school day," Chan explained. "We take attendance at every club, and we call the parents if students don't show up."

The After-School Corporation, which provides grants, training and technical assistance to more than 100 community-based organizations in New York City to run after-school programs in schools, encourages program directors to work with principals to select professional development programs for after-school staff that will also be of interest to school staff. To learn more about TASC and professional development strategies for after-school, visit www.tascorp.org.

"There are a lot of schools that are operating quality child-care programs, but not after-school programs."

Sue Masterson, Principal Monroe Elementary School Janesville, Wisconsin

Along with structured professional development time, principals should also encourage teachers and after-school staff members to spend time together more informally to help build relationships.

Inviting teachers to visit after-school programs and welcoming teachers into classes is one way to encourage familiarity. Another is hosting a pizza party after school or organizing a trip to a baseball game so that teachers and after-school staff members can meet and get to know each other in a casual setting.

After-school programs often draw upon a mix of paraprofessionals, certified teachers, volunteers and college interns to lead activities. All of these diverse staff should have opportunities to build relationships with each other that will ultimately make them a stronger team.

FOCUS ON PRACTICE

Building Confidence for School and Life

Carol Miller, Principal
John B. McFerran Elementary School, Louisville, Kentucky

Standing beside one of the most notorious housing projects in Louisville, John B. McFerran Elementary School provides students with a sanctuary from the crime and violence outside its doors.

Principal Carol Miller, who has led the 980-student school for 25 years, knows most of the parents of her students worry about their children having safe and enriching environments. She has worked hard to build a range of quality programs that provide students and families with academic and social support during the school year and into the summer months.

After-school programs evolved slowly at McFerran, a pre-K-5 school that, under a state-managed choice plan, has created an even balance of white and black students. In the beginning, the only after-school activity was a baseball team. As Miller became more astute at identifying after-school funds, and as Kentucky's landmark education reform act provided schools with family resource coordinators, after-school activities expanded. Today, more than 300 students a year participate in one of the school's after-school activities.

These include a science club, a computer club, soccer and basketball teams, cheerleading, girls' and boys' clubs and academic tutoring. The school's family resource coordinator also serves as the after-school coordinator.

"The coordinator is here during the day so he understands what the kids are studying," says Miller. "We try to make as many connections between school and after-school as we can."

For example, the after-school coordinator brought students and parents on a tour of an art museum to expose them to cultural and artistic work that complements and enhances their understanding of what the students are learning in class. There are also popular "night hikes" in the forest where students have the opportunity to understand scientific and environmental issues in a more practical way. During the summer, students have access to academic support in the morning and recreational and leisure activities in the afternoon. The school also provides GED classes and English language classes for parents.

Above all, Miller wants after-school programs to help develop young people who are well-rounded and confident.

"For us, after-school is about social skills, learning how to get along and live in this world and solve problems," says Miller. "School can be stressful now, especially with high-stakes testing. Students need some down time. Not everyone is good at academics, and every student needs something they can feel successful doing and come back to school feeling better."

Suggested Elements of an Ideal After-School Homework Program

To improve academic achievement:

- The program sets aside **time** for the completion of homework assignments. A schedule is available for when homework can be completed; this can run simultaneously with other program activities.
- The program sets aside **space** for the completion of homework assignments. A space is clearly marked as an area where homework can be completed away from other competing activities; only homework is done there and students can enter only once.
- The program provides **materials** needed for the successful completion of assignments, such as paper, pencils, pens, rulers, calculators and computers. Tools are available that support independent learning, such as reference works, study guides, test preparation materials and access to homework hotlines.
- Staff members view homework as an important element within an active learning environment. They are trained to understand the importance of adult roles meant to motivate and mentor, and to monitor the homework process. Staff members have skills needed to assist students with proper homework behavior.
- The program has mechanisms that help participants focus their attention on academic tasks; homework or learning contracts and logs are used to track homework completion.
- The program provides opportunities to use non-staff resources to help with homework assignments; cross-age, peer and adult volunteer tutoring are available.
- The program provides study or learning opportunities for students without homework or completed assignments. Alternative activities related to the acquisition of academic skills might include high-interest reading materials, test study groups, test practice areas, math games, art materials

To improve non-academic behaviors related to academic success:

- The program includes developing student study skills during time separate from homework time; staff members teach students to track assignments, to use resource materials, etc.
- The program includes training in time-management skills; participants are taught how to plan their time.
- The program fosters self-direction, self-discipline, inquisitiveness, independent problem-solving. Adult supervisors are trained in techniques for helping with homework; study skills that can be taught to students; and basic techniques for taking tests. Participants are taught when and how to seek assistance.

Reprinted with permission from Harris Cooper, Ph.D., Duke University, Program in Education.

QUESTIONS FOR FURTHER REFLECTION

Ensure that the school's learning and core academic standards are connected to activities in after-school programs.

- Does school staff share our learning and academic standards with the program director and after-school staff members?
- Are those standards reflected in after-school program activities?
- Are after-school program goals shared with school staff members?
- Do after school and school staff members have the opportunity to work alongside each other as committee members, for example, or as tutors or teachers?

Offer learning opportunities in after-school that are different from, but connected to, those in the school day.

- Are after-school and school day programs complementary?
- How are they different?
- Do students perceive the after-school program as "more school"?
- What are some of the ways in which after-school activities are connected to school-day activities?

Provide a continuum of services and supports for students.

- What range of services and supports does the after-school program offer—homework assistance, enrichment activities, tutoring, extra-curricular clubs, service and civic development opportunities, mentoring, arts, technology and foreign language lessons?
- Do students receive healthy snacks?
- Do students have access to services and supports they need most?
- Do students have access to activities that are fun and challenging?
- Are after-school staff members appropriately qualified?

Connect professional development opportunities for after-school and school-day staff members to ensure consistency in standards of teaching and learning and to encourage relationship-building among staff members.

- Are after-school staff members embraced as equal partners in students' learning and development?
- Do I look for professional development opportunities that will serve both staffs?
- Do I look for professional development opportunities that will help students academically, socially and emotionally?
- Do I look for professional development opportunities that involve lessons and activities teachers and after-school staff members can develop and implement cooperatively?
- Do I look for professional development opportunities that address problems and challenges in integrating school and after-school learning?
- Do we have informal ways to build collegiality between staffs?

PLANNING TOOL

This assessment is designed to help you and your leadership team reflect periodically on your school practice. Look back at your answers to the Questions for Further Reflection as you complete the tool. Take the assessment at the beginning, middle and end of the year to track your progress. Note things you want to change or are doing well.

Once you have mastered an item, shift your focus to other items. You may add to the assessment if you discover additional indicators you would like to track. If a question is not applicable, leave it blank. Rate each question from 1 to 4: **1** Not at all, **2** Sometimes, **3** Most of the time, **4** Always

Ensure that the school's learning and core academic standards are connected to activities in after-school programs.	Beginning Rating	Middle Rating	End Rating
School learning and academic standards are shared with after-school program staff.			
School standards are reflected in after-school activities.			
School staff members are aware of after-school program goals.			
School and after-school staffs work with each other as committee members, tutors or teachers.			
Offer learning opportunities in after-school that are different from, but connected to, those in the school day.			
School and after-school programs are complementary.			
School and after-school programs are different.			
Students do not perceive the after-school program as more school.			
After-school learning opportunities are clearly connected to school-day learning.			

Provide a continuum of services and supports for students.	Beginning Rating	Middle Rating	End Rating
The after-school program offers a range of services and supports for students, including:			
homework assistance			
enrichment activities			
mentoring			
healthy snacks			
Students have access to the services and supports they need most.			
Activities are fun.			
Activities are challenging.			
After-school staff members are appropriately qualified.			
Connect professional development opportunities for after-school and school-day staff members to ensure consistency in standards of teaching and learning and to encourage relationship-building among staff members.			
I look for professional development opportunities that will serve both school and after-school staff members.			
The program director and I work together to connect in school and after-school professional development opportunities.			
After-school staff members are embraced as equal partners in students' learning and development.			
There are informal ways for school and after-school staffs to build collegiality.			

Notes:

FOR MORE INFORMATION

Resources From NAESP

Jordan-Meldrum, J. *Making the Most of After-School Time: Ten Case Studies of School-Based After-School Programs.* Alexandria, VA: National Association of Elementary School Principals, 2005.

Noam, G. "After-School Education: What Principals Should Know." *Principal, Beyond the Bell,* Vol. 82. No. 5. May/June 2003.

On the Web

The Children's Aid Society (www.childrensaidsociety.org) guides underserved children and families toward cutting-edge after-school programs and community services. The programs use a range of curricula designed to help students' literacy, mathematics, science and leadership skills.

Just Think (www.justthink.org) develops and delivers effective curricula and innovative programs that build skills in critical thinking and creative media production.

National Institute on Out-of-School Time (www.niost.org) works to ensure that all children, youth and families have access to high-quality programs, activities and opportunities during non-school hours.

National Partnership for Quality Afterschool Learning (www.sedl.org/afterschool) builds local capacity to provide rich academic content through engaging and challenging activities and to demonstrate the impact of academic programming on student outcomes. Its *Afterschool Training Kit* provides tools, models and expertise to improve after-school learning nationwide.

Promising Practices in Afterschool Listserv (www.afterschool.org/ppas_listserv.cfm) is a virtual community of after-school program staff, youth workers, school-age care providers, educators, researchers, policymakers and others with an interest in keeping up-to-date on the latest in after-school.

Promising Practices Network (www.promisingpractices.net) provides quality, evidence-based information about what works to improve the lives of children, youth and families.

From the Research

Bouffard, S. and Little, P. "Promoting Quality Through Professional Development: A Framework for Evaluation." *Issue and Opportunities in Out-of-School Time Evaluation,* No. 8. August 2004.

Cooper, H. M. *The Battle Over Homework: Common Ground for Administrators, Teachers and Parents* (2nd Ed.). Thousand Oaks, CA: Corwin Press, 2001.

Gardner, H. *Multiple Intelligences: The Theory in Practice.* New York: Basic Books, 1993.

Reisner, E., White, R., Russell, C. and Birmingham, J. *Building Quality, Scale and Effectiveness in After-School Programs.* Washington, DC: Policy Studies Associates, 2004.

5

Evaluation

Work with program directors to evaluate after-school programs to ensure they achieve defined outcomes.

After-school initiatives set goals across a wide range of areas that include student engagement, youth development and academic performance. Specific feedback on whether programs are meeting desired outcomes is crucial to informed decision-making. Assessments can help principals maintain continuous improvement, address weaknesses and support efforts to make the case for after-school programs to policymakers, funders and the broader community.

In an era of accountability, schools and students are expected more than ever before to demonstrate academic progress against rigorous standards. After-school programs are not exempt from the accountability pressures. They must prove they can make a positive impact in this results-based environment if they hope to win the confidence of education and political leaders grappling with competing demands and shrinking resources.

After-school programs that can clearly prove effectiveness across a range of different measures stand out by showcasing the effect they have on students, families, schools and neighborhoods.

Data collected to evaluate programs can serve other purposes as well. Evaluations of quality programs provide information on best practices that can guide new programs and provide new ideas to reenergize existing programs. Evaluations also keep after-school programs focused and strategic in how they respond to the needs of students, parents and community members.

Principals who evaluate after-school programs to ensure they achieve defined outcomes:

- Define short- and long-term outcomes for after-school programs collaboratively with the program director
- Use data to ensure that children most in need have access to after-school
- Work with the program director to identify, generate and collect data to assess after-school programs
- Encourage the use of data and best practices to improve programs by fostering communication about results among teachers, program directors, after-school staff members and other stakeholders
- Use data and evaluation results to document program impact and make the case for quality after-school programs with school, community and political leaders

Define short- and long-term outcomes for after-school programs collaboratively with the program director.

Principals and program directors should meet before activities begin to determine what specific outcomes programs will be expected to produce. Evaluations will not be meaningful unless there is a clear understanding up front about what the goals are for after-school activities. Expectations should be set high, but must also be practical and measurable given the resources and capacity of the program.

Not all outcomes will emerge over the same period of time. If an after-school program has a science fiction or fantasy book club, for example, program directors and principals may set a goal to have all students read three books every two months. This goal can be measured in the short term by having students log their reflections and summaries in a personal portfolio where they are encouraged to express themselves creatively through poetry, artwork or essays. A six-month goal could include having students write short stories of their own that they share with other students. At the end of the year, students might be expected to have read between 15 and 20 books and to have several forms of writing responses in their personal portfolios.

Other after-school outcomes may include deepening student engagement or helping immigrant parents who speak English as a second language feel more comfortable dealing with school officials. These outcomes will take more time to evaluate effectively, and these challenges should be considered when defining goals.

Principals and program directors should write down goals, share them with school staff members and encourage feedback from teachers on how outcomes can be best reached by working together.

Checklist for Evaluations

- Develop an evaluation plan that describes program goals, strategies for achieving outcomes and a timetable for implementation and results
- Invite stakeholders into the evaluation process by considering shared goals
- Focus data collection on key areas that are integral to the program's success
- If possible, use outside evaluators with research experience to ensure accuracy, lack of bias and sound research principles

Source: The After-School Corporation

Use data to ensure that children most in need have access to after-school.

All students can benefit from the support that quality after-school settings provide young people. However, in too many cases, children living in poverty, recent immigrants with limited English skills and students with severe academic challenges have the least access to after-school experiences..

National surveys show that minority parents, in particular, have a harder time than other parents finding structured programs for their children after school—and are less satisfied with the programs they do find.

Effective principals and program directors recognize that access to after-school opportunities should be equitable, and they use data to ensure that students who can most benefit from the added value of after-school are doing so. Just as the use of data and targeted resources in high-performing, high-poverty schools has helped narrow achievement gaps among students of different racial and socioeconomic backgrounds, data on access to after-school experiences can also begin to bridge gaps in opportunity and performance.

Working together with program directors, principals might consider:

- Surveying students eligible for federal free or reduced-price lunch to see who is not currently participating in after-school activities
- Using data collected to meet federal No Child Left Behind mandates to see which students would most benefit from after-school tutoring and enrichment
- Reviewing attendance and discipline records to identify students who are chronically truant from school or causing disruptions in class as potential participants in after-school activities

"Principals play an important role in selecting and generating data about what's working in after-school programs."

Jodi Grant
Afterschool Alliance

Work with the program director to identify, generate and collect data to assess after-school programs.

Principals and program directors realize gathering targeted information about after-school activities is an integral component to ensuring high-quality after-school experiences. To this end, it is important that the process of data collection is strategic and coordinated to identify information about key outcomes. The following data collection methods are often used to gather information on students' use of out-of-school time.

"The goal for our after-school program was to increase students' opportunities and assume a greater role in educating children at schools. Our students' test scores rose considerably. We know that after-school is a big part of that. We're reaching kids that we have never reached before."

Pat Echanis,
Principal
Parkdale Elementary
Parkdale, Oregon

Surveys and questionnaires are effective ways to gather specific information from students, staff members, families, community members and other stakeholders. Data collected often includes demographic information, satisfaction levels and opinions about the program.

Interviews and focus groups are most often used to gather detailed, qualitative descriptions of how programs operate and how stakeholders perceive them; interviews are typically conducted one-on-one. Focus groups are best conducted in small groups. Questions asked are generally open-ended and responses are documented in thorough, detailed notes or transcription.

Observation is an unobtrusive method for gathering information. Observations can be highly structured, with protocols for recording specific behaviors, or unstructured, by taking a "fly on the wall" approach. They are most reliable when conducted over a period of time. Evaluations can include observation of peer interactions, staff-participant interactions and evidence of youth autonomy and decision-making.

Collecting data before a program begins and comparing it with data gathered at different points throughout the program implementation provides information on progress or trouble spots. It can also suggest the effect of the after-school program on outcomes. A more sophisticated data-collection model is needed to help prove causal relationships between after-school programs and results. This may require the use of control groups and an ability to gauge whether other factors besides after-school contributed to gains.

While academic improvement is an important outcome to measure, many after-school programs also aim more broadly to help young people develop self-confidence, interpersonal skills and cultural understanding and appreciation. These characteristics may be harder to capture with numerical data, but they are critical to after-school experiences and can be evaluated in more qualitative ways through focused observations, personal interviews with students and structured focus groups.

FOCUS ON PRACTICE

Putting Evaluation Results to Work

Patrick Bryan, Principal
Jackson Preparatory Magnet School, St. Paul, Minnesota

Located in Frogtown, a racially mixed neighborhood in St. Paul, Jackson Magnet School serves a diverse population of over 500 students. Fifty-five percent of students are Asian—most are Hmong—70 percent speak a language other than English at home and 88 percent qualify for free or reduced-price lunch.

When Patrick Bryan arrived at Jackson in 2000, he learned that his after-school program, funded by 21st Century Community Learning Centers, was in trouble. The after-school coordinator at the time had overspent her budget and alienated many of the school's community partners.

Bryan worked with Lee Litman, St. Paul's 21st CCLC coordinator, to hire a new after-school coordinator and immediately set about repairing relationships with community groups.

"I wanted to involve as many community groups as possible, to draw on the resources of the Frogtown neighborhood," notes Bryan. "My goal was to build a program that would complement the acceleration and enrichment focus of the school. I also knew that it was important to demonstrate that the after-school program was really helping the kids and families who needed it most."

Data provided the way. A multi-site evaluation conducted by the Center for Applied Research and Educational Improvement at the University of Minnesota found that Jackson's after-school participants received higher scores than their non-participating counterparts on standardized tests. Teachers reported that "four out of every five students showed improved habits and skills consistently associated with better academic performance, classroom behavior and improved academic work." Additionally, the researchers found that after-school "was an integrated program." In other words, in-school and after-school were not seen as separate, but simply parts of the larger school offering.

Bryan and the current after-school coordinator, Emily Weiss, have used data from the CAREI report and other evaluations conducted by local partners to make changes to the multi-faceted program, creating more room for student input, for example. Today, the program serves 200 students and offers activities such as Hmong Youth Pride, 4H Youth Development, Success for All tutoring, homework assistance and music lessons.

Bryan has also used evaluation results to build support for the program and the school with parents and the broader community. When faced with impending budget cuts recently, Bryan sent out a survey to parents. Without listing specifics, he asked parents to list the three services they would like to see remain in the school. After-school was by far the most frequently mentioned service parents wanted to see remain in the building.

TOOLS YOU CAN USE

Developing a Theory of Change

A theory of change is a progression of thinking and planning that guides a team toward setting program goals and designing program elements that can result in positive participant outcomes. Developing a theory of change is also useful for evaluation planning, continuous learning and improvement and effective communication among diverse program partners.

The first step in developing a theory of change is to draw a logic model. A logic model summarizes the key elements of a program, identifies the rationale behind the elements, articulates short- and long-term outcomes and how they can be measured and shows the cause-and-effect relationships between a program and its desired outcomes.

Logic Model: A Visual Representation of a Theory of Change

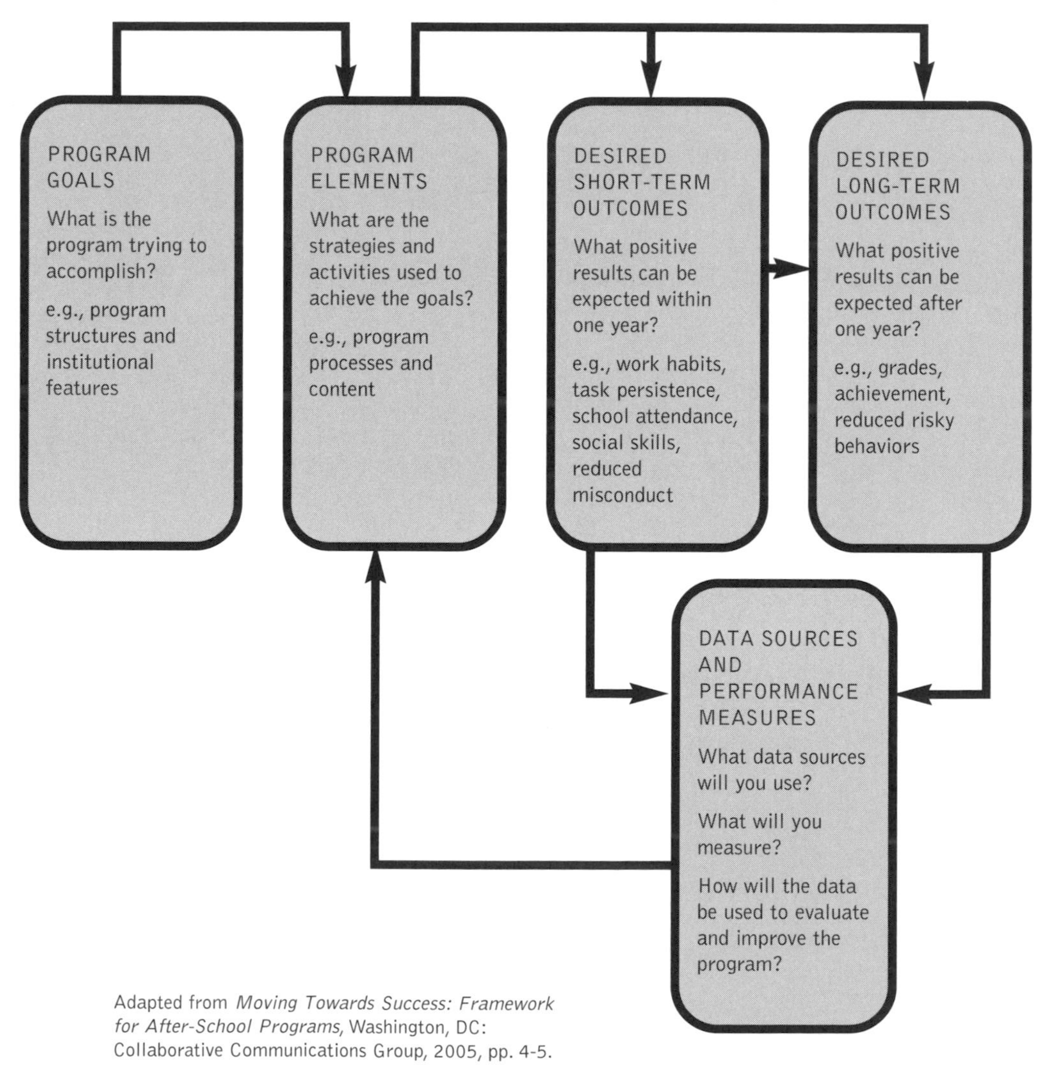

Adapted from *Moving Towards Success: Framework for After-School Programs,* Washington, DC: Collaborative Communications Group, 2005, pp. 4-5.

Encourage the use of data and best practices to improve programs by fostering communication about results among teachers, program directors, after-school staff members and other stakeholders.

Effective principals regularly use data for program improvement in their schools. They also set a climate in their buildings that encourages the use of data for decision-making. This climate extends to after-school programs as well.

Principals collect and use a wealth of data on student progress—grades, retention rates and attendance, for example. By sharing this information with after-school staff members, principals can enable them to tailor their programs to student needs more effectively.

By encouraging both the collection of data on after-school program effectiveness and the sharing of this data with stakeholders, principals can help ensure that decisions are informed by relevant information. After-school data can also identify for principals areas for improvement in the school-day program.

Principals and program directors should consider meeting with school and after-school staff members every few months to think systematically about how data is being put to use.

Use data and evaluation results to document program impact and make the case for quality after-school programs with school, community and political leaders.

Data can be used to tell a story. Principals and after-school leaders recognize the potential of framing data as a compelling narrative to help persuade leaders that after-school initiatives are worthy investments.

School board members, community groups, philanthropic organizations and political leaders want tangible and accessible results that capture the essence of why after-school matters. Principals begin to make the case for sustainable after-school programs when they work with program directors to:

- Consistently present data findings on the academic and social-emotional benefits of after-school during school board meetings and other district gatherings
- Share data with civic organizations that highlights how after-school has helped students become more active participants in the community
- Create informational packets or brochures that synthesize data results into an easy-to-read format and share them with school staff, parents, political leaders and community members
- Pitch story ideas to local media that use both hard data and anecdotal evidence to showcase after-school successes

When principals and program directors package data for the public, they should include an executive summary that clearly describes what outcomes were evaluated and the methods used to collect information. Highlighting key findings gives readers a snapshot of the most important data. Creative display is also helpful. Photographs of participants, along with charts or graphics that accentuate important themes, can tell more than 1,000 words.

FOCUS ON PRACTICE

Using Evaluation as a Tool for Making Programs Fun and Rigorous

Joy Lea, Principal
Cashman Middle School, Las Vegas, Nevada

"We serve over 1,100 6th, 7th and 8th graders at Cashman Middle School," explains Principal Joy Lea, "and I would like to see every one of them participate in our after-school program."

Cashman's after-school program, which currently reaches 400 students, is anchored by a group of partners that includes 21st Century Community Learning Centers; GEAR-UP—Gaining Early Awareness and Readiness for Undergraduate Programs—a federally funded effort designed to prepare at-risk middle and high school students to enter and succeed in post-secondary education; and Las Vegas' After-School All Stars, a national program that engages students in sports and academic activities.

Known as "Moomba: Let's All Get Together and Have a Great Time," the Cashman after-school program umbrella offers activities ranging from computer games and hip-hop dance to intensive reading and math programs, along with soccer and boxing and a "mad scientist" club. Since the Cashman student population is highly transitory—44 percent leave each year—and over half of the students are in the English Learner Program, Moomba programs are targeted to reach students who need them most.

Through its partnership with After-School All Stars, Cashman participates in a Quality Assurance System assessment. "The great thing about this evaluation system," notes Lea, "is that it is very comprehensive." Developed by Foundations, Inc., QAS looks at issues such as staffing, facilities, health and safety, as well as "program-focused building blocks" such as program mission, target population and activities.

Lea and after-school partners used the QAS assessment feedback from 2004-05 to make several changes to the 2005-06 Moomba program. Now, for example, children have down time every day to socialize and have a snack before they enter the "power hour," the academic segment of the program. Cashman is also hiring teachers from the community to help with teacher burnout, a problem uncovered in the assessment. "Finding the right teacher is the key to almost everything," says Lea. "Kids respond and connect to good teachers."

"We've seen our enrollment in the after-school program double this year," explains Lea. "In part, this is due to our ability to use the assessment as a program planning tool. My goal is to serve as many kids as possible and to do that as effectively as possible. I can only see the program growing over the next few years. It's very exciting!"

QUESTIONS FOR FURTHER REFLECTION

Define short- and long-term outcomes for after-school programs collaboratively with the program director.

- Have we developed a framework for evaluating after-school programs?
- Do I meet with the program director to discuss what outcomes the program should be expected to produce?
- Do we need to hire an external evaluator?
- Have we identified clear and achievable short- and long-term outcomes?
- Do we periodically review and, if necessary, revise outcomes?

Use data to ensure that children most in need have access to after-school.

- Have I reviewed data to determine what students' after-school needs are?
- Does our team know which students are attending after-school?
- Are we reaching students who might not otherwise have access to enrichment or homework assistance?
- Are we reaching students who need additional tutoring assistance or guidance?
- Are we reaching students who would benefit the most from after-school programs?

Work with the program director to identify, generate and collect data to assess after-school programs.

- Have I met with the program director to identify important data and discuss data-collection methods?
- Does our school team give the after-school program access to relevant school data?
- Are we ensuring the integrity of school data; is students' privacy protected?
- If the after-school program contracts with an external evaluator, do we meet with and monitor the evaluator?

Encourage the use of data and best practices to improve programs by fostering communication about results among teachers, program directors, after-school staff members and other stakeholders.

- Do I share data on student progress with after-school staff?
- Do I encourage after-school staff to collect and analyze data on program effectiveness?
- Do I facilitate communications among different stakeholders about the use of after-school data?
- Do I share program results with school staff? Other stakeholders?
- Have we used program evaluation results to modify school and after-school programs, if necessary?

Use data and evaluation results to document program impact and make the case for quality after-school programs with school, community and political leaders.

- Do we have access to relevant evaluation data?
- How do I and our school team use data to tell a story about the impact of after-school programs on students?
- Do I refer to program results when I make the case for after-school programs with school, community and political leaders?

PLANNING TOOL

This assessment is designed to help you and your leadership team reflect periodically on your school practice. Look back at your answers to the Questions for Further Reflection as you complete the tool. Take the assessment at the beginning, middle and end of the year to track your progress. Note things you want to change or are doing well.

Once you have mastered an item, shift your focus to other items. You may add to the assessment if you discover additional indicators you would like to track. If a question is not applicable, leave it blank. Rate each question from 1 to 4: **1** Not at all, **2** Sometimes, **3** Most of the time, **4** Always

Define short- and long-term outcomes for after-school programs collaboratively with the program director.	Beginning Rating	Middle Rating	End Rating
The program director and I have established a framework for evaluating the after-school program.			
The program has clear short-term outcomes.			
The program has clear long-term outcomes.			
Outcomes are achievable.			
We consult with an external evaluator, when necessary.			
The program director and I periodically review and, if necessary, revise outcomes.			
Use data to ensure that children most in need have access to after-school.			
We review data (grades, test scores, free and reduced-price lunch data, teacher feedback) to determine which students would most benefit from after-school programs.			
We encourage those students to participate.			
We track which students actually participate.			

Work with the program director to identify, generate and collect data to assess after-school programs.	Beginning Rating	Middle Rating	End Rating
The program director and I identify what data need to be collected and how it will be collected.			
If necessary, we work with an external evaluator to determine data collection needs.			
Members of my school team and I give the after-school program director and external evaluator access to relevant school data.			
We ensure the integrity of school data (i.e., students' privacy is protected).			
If there is an external evaluator, the program director and I meet with and monitor the evaluator.			
Encourage the use of data and best practices to improve programs by fostering communication about results among teachers, program directors, after-school staff members and other stakeholders.			
I facilitate communications among stakeholders about the use of after-school data to improve the program.			
I share program results with school staff.			
We share program results with other stakeholders.			
We use program evaluation results to improve school programs, where appropriate.			
Use data and evaluation results to document program impact and make the case for quality after-school programs with school, community and political leaders.			
Members of my school team and I have access to relevant program evaluation data.			
We use data to document the impact of after-school programming.			
We use data to make the case for after-school programming with school, community and political leaders.			

FOR MORE INFORMATION

Resources From NAESP

Bell, M. "Are After-School Programs Accountable?" *Principal, Beyond the Bell*, Vol. 82, No. 5. May/June 2003.

Owens, D. "Eight Keys to a Successful Expanded Day Program." *Principal, Beyond the Bell*, Vol. 82, No. 5. May/June 2003.

On the Web

Academy for Educational Development (www.aed.org/Education/US/afterschool.cfm) partners with schools to develop promising practices and after-school assessments.

The **Foundations, Inc.** (qas.foundationsinc.org) Quality Assessment System allows practitioners to evaluate and improve their after-school programs.

Harvard Family Research Project (www.gse.harvard.edu/hfrp/projects/afterschool/evaldatabase.html) Out-of-School Time Evaluation Database is a compilation of profiles of OST programs and initiatives. It provides accessible information about evaluation work of both large and small OST programs to support the development of high-quality evaluations and programs in the out-of-school time field.

From the Research

C. S. Mott Foundation Committee on After-School Research and Practice. *Moving Towards Success: Framework for After-School Programs.* Washington, DC: Collaborative Communications Group, 2005.

Center for Applied Research and Evaluation, University of Minnesota. *Final Evaluation Report: 21st Century Community Learning Centers Pathways to Progress, St. Paul Public Schools.* Minneapolis, MN: March 2004.

Lewis, A. and Paik, S. *Add It Up: Using Research To Improve Education for Low-Income and Minority Students.* Washington, DC: Poverty & Race Research Action Council, 2001.

Reisner, E. R. *Using Evaluation Methods To Promote Continuous Improvement and Accountability in After-School Programs: A Guide.* Washington, DC: Policy Studies Associates, 2004.

6 Champion After-School

Promote access to high-quality after-school programs for all children

If young people are going to participate in enriching after-school programs, they need enthusiastic ambassadors and savvy advocates for extended learning opportunities.

Currently, the voices of principals are often not heard when policymakers, researchers and youth advocates gather at the local, state and federal levels to discuss after-school initiatives. By filling largely untapped roles as champions of after-school, principals can help ensure that these programs are linked to the school's vision, are adequately funded and serve the needs of all students.

Young people are looking for structured activities when the school day ends. Surveys show that students report feeling more engaged with school when they are involved with after-school programs. Demand for after-school, however, far outstrips supply. While there has been a significant push in recent years to ensure that all students have the opportunity to take part in after-school programs, low-income urban areas and isolated rural communities remain underserved. English language learners and special needs students with physical and mental challenges also often lack quality after-school programs. Lack of transportation, participation fees and a lack of community partners in depressed areas all play a role in limiting access.

Principals who are at the table speaking out about the value of after-school opportunities convey a powerful message to school boards, city councils, foundations, community groups and the media that after-school is not a luxury, but an integral component of educating and supporting children and families.

Principals who promote access to high-quality after-school programs for all children:

- Use the credibility of the principal to advocate for after-school programs for students
- Understand after-school funding streams and policy issues
- Keep the public and policymakers focused on the need for a continuum of services that supports students' learning beyond the school day
- Promote and facilitate partnerships among schools, providers and communities that secure adequate, sustainable funding for after-school programs

Use the credibility of the principal to advocate for after-school programs for students.

Effective principals recognize that as school and community leaders they are uniquely positioned to influence how a broad range of educational, civic and political leaders view after-school. Parents, teachers, students and policymakers all look to principals to articulate a school's priorities and to outline the ingredients needed to make a school community successful. Principals can use their positions to advocate for after-school programs by:

- Using the school newsletter and Web site to advertise and advocate for quality after-school programs
- Encouraging the school's PTA to become vocal advocates of after-school activities
- Providing after-school literature to parents of new students when they enroll and setting up a table prominently displaying after-school programs during back-to-school night
- Promoting *Lights On Afterschool* and other events involving community leaders
- Honoring after-school staff and participants at school assemblies and award ceremonies
- Inviting local media to visit effective after-school programs

Understand after-school funding streams and policy issues.

"Follow the money" is a well-known axiom of reporters and detectives hot on a trail. Principals will also do well to know where dollars can be tapped to start and sustain after-school programs.

Knowing how to access funds for after-school programs is challenging work. The only federal funding source dedicated solely to after-school programs is the 21st Century Community Learning Centers program, which directs funds to schools in need of improvement or schools with high concentrations of low-income students. But other federal sources of funds may be available.

The No Child Left Behind Act provides several opportunities for funding for after-school programs. Because the law seeks to close achievement gaps between students of different races and ethnicities, after-school programs that want access to NCLB funds must demonstrate research-based results that show how after-school programs are improving student achievement or removing barriers to academic success.

Principals might consider the following options for tapping federal funds under the law:

- Title I funding under NCLB encourages the use of extended day, extended year and summer programs to increase learning time
- After-school programs are eligible to become supplemental education service providers under an NCLB provision that requires schools not making adequate yearly progress for three years to offer low-income students additional academic support outside of school
- After-school programs with mentoring, character education or drug and violence prevention components are eligible for NCLB funding under the Safe and Drug-Free Schools and Communities program
- After-school programs with service learning, counseling and parental and community involvement can apply for funding under the Innovative Programs section of NCLB designed to encourage innovation and creativity in improving student achievement

One of the greatest challenges many after-school programs face is building a sustainable funding base. One effective strategy for addressing this is to work with program directors to create a broad-based community advisory board that can help develop long-term support for your program. This board can help principals and program directors access funds, resources and support on an ongoing basis.

"After-school has become an answer to declining resources during the school day. Principals need to look at what they have to work with, and how they can manage different pieces and funding streams to make the program better for students."

Bonnie Tryon, Principal Golding Elementary School Cobleskill, New York

"Principals have a significant role in forming changes in 21st Century Community Learning Center legislation. They can demonstrate how significant the funding is for schools and students."

Carol Mitchell
21st Century Community Learning Centers
U.S. Department of Education

Building a Sustainable Funding Base

As principals and program directors look for funding to support and sustain after-school funding, they should consider the following points:

- How much will the program cost on an annual basis? Costs include start-up costs, planning and facilities development, salaries and benefits for staff, curriculum and materials, transportation, food and field trips.
- How will those costs be covered? What expenses can be paid for by school or district budgets, partnering agencies, grants and contributions from local businesses?
- How will the program be sustained over time? Once initial grants and other funds have been obtained, who will be responsible for monitoring and securing funding? Will there be a fundraising team or an advisory board?

School leaders should also have a good relationship with the school district's government affairs and communications offices to remain updated on current legislation and new legislative initiatives related to extended day programs. Building alliances with lobbying groups that are already experienced in promoting youth development efforts can also help principals strengthen their positions as champions of after-school.

Keep the public and policymakers focused on the need for a continuum of services that supports students' learning beyond the school day.

Principals strive to keep after-school learning high on the public and policy agenda by:

- Testifying before council meetings, board of education sessions and legislative committee hearings to advocate for quality extended day programs
- Inviting political leaders and lawmakers to visit after-school activities
- Meeting with the Chamber of Commerce, civic associations and local religious groups to educate a diverse range of community members about the need for learning beyond the school day
- Participating with other community advocates in school district budget proposal meetings to ensure after-school programs are well funded
- Writing columns or letters to the editor touting the advantages of after-school

The voices of principals also need to be heard at the state policy level. One potential avenue for principals is the National Network of Statewide Afterschool Networks. The network, funded by the Charles Stewart Mott Foundation, is a coalition of 31 states that helps bring together policymakers, educators, youth development workers and others in their collective mission to build partnerships and policies that are committed to the development and sustainability of quality after-school programs. Networks in these states raise awareness among governors, mayors and other key decision-makers about the impact after-school programs can have on student success.

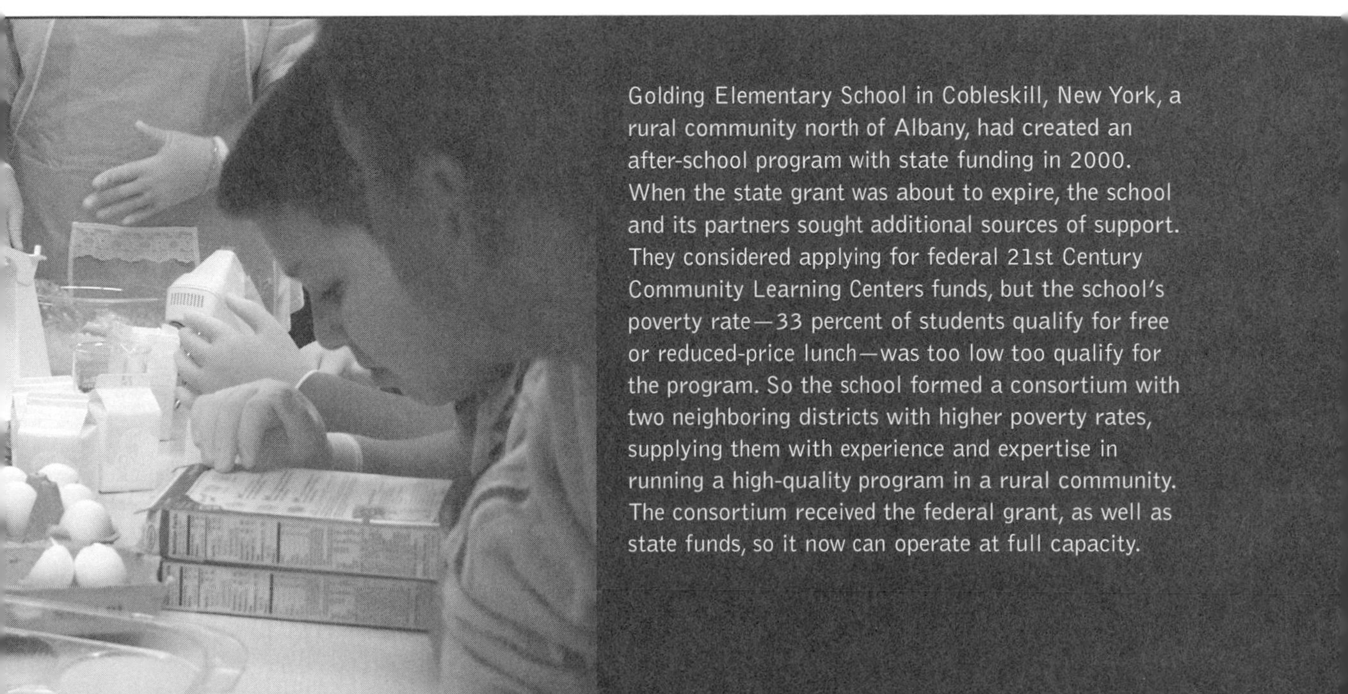

Golding Elementary School in Cobleskill, New York, a rural community north of Albany, had created an after-school program with state funding in 2000. When the state grant was about to expire, the school and its partners sought additional sources of support. They considered applying for federal 21st Century Community Learning Centers funds, but the school's poverty rate—33 percent of students qualify for free or reduced-price lunch—was too low too qualify for the program. So the school formed a consortium with two neighboring districts with higher poverty rates, supplying them with experience and expertise in running a high-quality program in a rural community. The consortium received the federal grant, as well as state funds, so it now can operate at full capacity.

Achieving Sustainability: Eight Critical Elements for Success

In order for after-school programs to make a difference in the lives of children and families over time, they must be built to last. Use this list of eight critical elements for success as a guide for developing and sustaining your program.

"Principals are a key connector. They can see what they need to make after-school work. Their voices are powerful when advocating for systematic changes, systematic policies and practices that can influence policy at local and state levels."

Ayeola Fortune
Council of Chief State School Officers

1. Vision: Having a clear-cut objective that articulates how an initiative's programs or activities will improve the lives of children, families and communities is one of the most important and basic steps involved in achieving sustainability. Without articulating these objectives and developing a plan for achieving them, no initiative can be truly viable.

2. Results: Demonstrating program success through measurable results (e.g., established indicators and performance measures) is crucial for building support from key stakeholders in the community. Stakeholder support, in turn, increases the likelihood of program continuance.

3. Strategic Financing: Developing a strategic financing orientation is critical for program leaders. It enables them to identify the resources they need to sustain their activities and then develop strategies to bring these resources together to achieve their goals.

4. Adaptability to Changing Conditions: Adjusting to changing social, economic and political trends in the community enables initiatives to take advantage of various opportunities that can help achieve sustainability. Making these adjustments also allows initiatives to identify and overcome any external threats that could obstruct program continuance.

This is a crucial element in building after-school programs that last. Funding streams change rapidly; administrations come and go, as do staff members. Successful after-school programs expect change and plan for it. They are strong, yet flexible. They continually look for ways to build buy-in and support, and they adapt when conditions change.

5. Broad Base of Community Support: Achieving a broad base of community support means determining who within the community supports an initiative, who needs it and who would care if it were gone. Often when an initiative is able to build a broad base of supporters who care about it and believe it is vital, fiscal and non-fiscal support will follow.

6. Key Champions: Rallying leaders from businesses, faith-based institutions, government and other parts of the community who are committed to an initiative's vision and are willing to use their power and prestige to generate support for that program will help to ensure long-term stability.

7. Strong Internal Systems: Building strong internal systems, such as fiscal management, accounting, information, personnel systems (e.g., professional development for after-school staff) and governance structures, enables an initiative to work effectively and efficiently. Establishing these systems also allows initiatives to document their results and demonstrate their soundness to potential funders.

8. Sustainability Plan: Creating sustainability plans, like business plans or strategic plans, helps initiative developers and managers clarify where they want their initiatives to go in the future. They provide benchmarks for determining whether initiatives are successfully reaching their goals. They also help policymakers, opinion leaders and investors decide whether and how to support certain initiatives.

Collectively, these elements are key to achieving a stable base of resources for community-based initiatives. Although all of the elements are important, it is not imperative to have all eight in place to achieve sustainability. The emphasis placed on each element and/or amount of time dedicated to a particular element will vary according to the needs and resources of the individual initiative or community.

"Sustaining Comprehensive Community Initiatives: Key Elements for Success," The Finance Project, *Finance Strategy Brief,* April 2002. Adapted with permission from The Finance Project.

Promote and facilitate partnerships among schools, providers and communities that secure adequate, sustainable funding for after-school programs.

After-school programs are typically funded by multiple sources. It is essential to have a range of funding options and to think strategically about financing after-school programs given the lack of a reliable funding stream. Effective principals act as champions for sustainable after-school funding by:

- Developing a sustainability plan that clearly articulates the need for a stable base of resources
- Building a broad base of community support by identifying key stakeholders who support the objectives of after-school
- Rallying leaders from businesses, faith-based institutions and government who can be powerful allies in securing sustainable funding

Lights On Afterschool is a nationwide program to call attention to the importance of after-school programs for America's children, families and communities. A project of the Afterschool Alliance—a nonprofit organization dedicated to ensuring that all children have access to quality, affordable after-school programs by 2010—*Lights On Afterschool* takes place at thousands of schools, community centers and public venues across the country each October. To obtain resources for planning a *Lights On* event in your school or community, visit the Afterschool Alliance Web site, www.afterschoolalliance.org.

FOCUS ON PRACTICE

Championing After-School Inside and Outside the School Building

Karina Constantino, Principal
Public School 22, Staten Island, New York

After meeting Karina Constantino at a community outreach event nine years ago, New York YMCA staff members worked with the principal to set up a Virtual Y after-school program in her school, PS 22—a pre-K-5 school with more than 1,100 students located on the North Shore of Staten Island. Since then, Constantino has been the program's biggest booster.

Constantino interviewed and helped select the original program director (who is now one of her assistant principals). She and her assistant principals stayed after school every day to make sure that the program ran smoothly. She also found ways for her teaching and support staff members—who were initially resistant to the program—to be involved by encouraging them to cooperatively develop curriculum with after-school staff members and to teach in some of the programs.

"Whatever I provided to my staff, I provided to the director and staff at the Y as well—school regulations, notes I took at meetings, professional development opportunities, you name it," notes Constantino. "Our goal was to speak with one voice, and it worked."

For Constantino, the after-school Y is a natural for the school. She notes that the school is ethnically diverse, with a recent influx of Middle Eastern immigrants. The after-school program provides the kind of safe environment she remembers from her own childhood, while at the same time providing enriching learning opportunities and engaging parents. "I am a product of the New York public schools," she says. "When I was growing up, school was the hub of community activity. I wanted to create an environment like that in our school, and the Y program has allowed me to do that."

Constantino's work has paid off. Nine years after the initial partnership began, the Virtual Y is still going strong at PS 22. Parents try to get their children into the school because of the after-school program. Recently, Constantino received a visit from a former student, now editor of *Time for Kids.* She donated $25,000 to the program.

"I don't know what my school would be like without after-school," Constantino says. "It should be in every school."

FOCUS ON PRACTICE

Filling the Gaps With After-School Support

Pat Echanis, Principal

Parkdale Elementary School, Parkdale, Oregon

Surrounded by apple orchards and tucked amid the scenic backdrop of Mount Hood, Parkdale Elementary School sits in an idyllic rural community off the Columbia River.

The natural beauty belies the stark challenges that many Latino immigrants flocking here for employment face as migrant workers. Parkdale students often live in small cabins with other migrant families and leave school for extended periods of time during harvest seasons in Mexico and California.

Pat Echanis, the principal at this K-5 grade school, has recognized the potential of after-school programs to support the needs of his students. Over his eight years as principal, he has become a visible champion for extended day experiences.

"The after-school program has made one of the biggest differences for our kids," says Echanis. "When students miss class time, we have to play catch-up with academics. That is why after-school time is so critical."

The impetus for an after-school program began when Echanis and other school leaders realized that many students' family lives were so difficult that simply completing homework was often a major hurdle. Many of the students leave school at the end of the day for cramped homes without heat or parental supervision. Eighty percent qualify for federal free or reduced-price lunch. Providing after-school help for students, Echanis knew, was a priority he could not afford to ignore.

When an initial 21st Century Community Learning Centers grant ran out, the school district approached a local hospital for after-school funding. The hospital now pays for all the after-school funding in the district; at Parkdale, the funds support two instructional assistants who provide after-school homework help and academic enrichment.

Echanis credits after-school support with helping students make considerable improvements on state accountability assessments. Five years ago, for example, 61 percent of his students met state reading standards. Most recent data shows that 86 percent of students have met the standard. In mathematics benchmark exams, the percentage of students passing assessments jumped from 58 percent five years ago to 91 percent today.

The principal admits to having a hands-on approach to after-school programs and frequently stops by to observe and talk with students and staff. He also offers a free trip to the movies every nine weeks for students who have perfect attendance. "It's a way of telling the kids, I honor the time and effort you put in to make yourself better," he says.

Echanis is now looking to broaden the largely academic focus of Parkdale's after-school program. The school has applied for a federal grant that would enable him to offer more youth development components, including art and music enrichment, when the school day ends.

"It's not always about the students adjusting to school," he says. "Our school needs to adjust to our kids' needs. After-school is helping to fill the gaps."

QUESTIONS FOR FURTHER REFLECTION

Use the credibility of the principal to advocate for after-school programs for students.

- Am I an effective advocate for after-school programs?
- Do I promote after-school programs in the school newsletter and on the school Web site?
- Do I promote after-school programs to new parents and students at back-to-school night and other school events?
- Do I promote after-school programs to the PTA and similar organizations?
- Do I support and invite students, parents and community leaders to participate in events such as *Lights On Afterschool?*

Understand the after-school funding streams and policy issues.

- Are members of the after-school team and I knowledgeable about after-school funding sources at the local, state and federal levels?
- Do I work collaboratively with the program director to identify and, if possible, tap those sources?
- Am I familiar with after-school policy issues at the local, state and federal levels?

Keep the public and policymakers focused on the need for a continuum of services that supports students' learning beyond the school day.

- Am I a public advocate for after-school programs in my community?
- Do I work with other after-school advocates and policy makers to ensure adequate funding and support for after-school programs?
- Am I proactive about inviting community leaders to visit after-school programs in my school?
- Do I volunteer to testify at board of education, city council and legislative committee meetings about the importance of quality after-school programs?

Promote and facilitate partnerships between schools, providers and communities that secure adequate, sustainable funding for after-school programs.

- Does our after-school team have, or are we building, a sustainability plan?
- Have we engaged a community advisory board to help us develop the plan?
- Are we implementing the plan effectively?
- Do I and our after-school team work with other groups to build a sustainable funding base for after-school programs in our community?

PLANNING TOOL

This assessment is designed to help you and your leadership team reflect periodically on your school practice. Look back at your answers to the Questions for Further Reflection as you complete the tool. Take the assessment at the beginning, middle and end of the year to track your progress. Note things you want to change or are doing well.

Once you have mastered an item, shift your focus to other items. You may add to the assessment if you discover additional indicators you would like to track. If a question is not applicable, leave it blank. Rate each question from 1 to 4: **1** Not at all, **2** Sometimes, **3** Most of the time, **4** Always

Use the credibility of the principal to advocate for after-school programs for students.	Beginning Rating	Middle Rating	End Rating
I am an effective advocate for after-school programs.			
I promote after-school programs in:			
the school newsletter			
the school Web site			
with new parents and students			
at back-to-school night			
with the PTA and similar organizations			
I invite students, parents and community leaders to participate in events.			
Understand after-school funding streams and policy issues.			
Members of the after-school team and I have knowledge about after-school funding sources:			
local			
state			
federal			
I work collaboratively with the program director to identify and tap those sources.			
I am familiar with after-school policy issues:			
local			
statewide			
at the federal level			

Keep the public and policymakers focused on the need for a continuum of services that supports students' learning beyond the school day.	Beginning Rating	Middle Rating	End Rating
I advocate for after-school programs In my community.			
I work with other after-school advocates and policymakers to ensure adequate support for after-school programs.			
I invite community leaders to visit after-school programs in the school.			
I volunteer to testify at board of education, city council and legislative committee meetings about the importance of quality after-school programs.			
Promote and facilitate partnerships among schools, providers and communities that secure adequate, sustainable funding for after-school programs.			
Our after-school team is building a sustainability plan.			
A community advisory board is helping us develop the plan.			
We are implementing the plan effectively.			
Members of the after-school team and I are working with other groups to build a sustainable funding base for after-school programs in our community.			

NOTES:

FOR MORE INFORMATION

Resources From NAESP

Rinehart, J. "A New Day Begins After-School." *Principal, Beyond the Bell*, Vol. 82, No. 5. May/June 2003.

"Strategies for Sustaining Afterschool Programs." Prepared for the National Elementary School Principals Annual Convention in San Francisco, April 2004.

On the Web

Afterschool Alliance (www.afterschoolalliance.org) is a nonprofit organization dedicated to raising awareness of the importance of after-school programs and advocating for quality, affordable programs for all children.

The Finance Project (www.financeproject.org) helps public- and private-sector leaders finance and sustain initiatives that lead to better futures for children, families and communities.

The Forum for Youth Investment (www.forumforyouthinvestment.org) helps youth and adult leaders sustain quality after-school programs. The forum provides numerous resources, tools and services to help leaders sustain in-school and community-based programs.

National Network of Statewide Afterschool Networks (www.statewideafterschoolnetworks.net) provides resources, tools and announcements to the statewide after-school networks. Designed for network coordinators and their teams, the Web site contains password-protected access to network-specific resources, convenings, media and state information.

Youth Today Newspaper (www.youthtoday.org) is an independent, nationally distributed newspaper that is read by more than 70,000 professionals in the youth service field.

From the Research

Council of Chief State School Officers. *Using NCLB Funds To Support Extended Learning Time: Opportunities for Afterschool Programs.* Washington, DC: 2005.

Deich, S., Wegener, V. and Wright, E. "Using Title I To Support Out-of-School Time and Community School Initiatives." *Strategy Brief*, Vol. 2. No. 4. January 2002.

The Forum for Youth Investment. "After-School for All? Exploring Access and Equity in After-School Programs." *Out-of-School Time Policy Commentary*, Issue 4. July 2003.

National Center for Community Education. *Fact Sheets for Afterschool Funding.* San Francisco, CA: undated.

National School Boards Association. *Building and Sustaining After-School Programs: Successful Practices in School Board Leadership.* Alexandria, VA: 2005.

A Call to Action

NAESP believes that creating a seamless learning day is essential to support children's learning. The benefits of after-school are evident in student achievement, social interaction and safety. By most assessments, after-school programs make a positive difference in the lives of students and improve the climate for school success.

Policymakers, as well as principals, must focus on a continuum of teaching and learning for children. After-school programs provide a wonderful opportunity to expand a variety of enrichment opportunities—not just academics—beyond the school day.

Here are some ways that federal, state and local leaders can support the extension of learning beyond the school day:

1. Integrate after-school into the overall policy on education, youth and family. In any policy decision, the entirety of children's time, learning and lives should be addressed. Thus, discussions about policy on education, youth or family must include discussions about after-school.

2. Steer state principal associations toward becoming part of statewide efforts to further after-school. The voice of principals needs to be heard not just at the district level but also at the state level. One method is to become involved in the National Network of Statewide Afterschool Networks. This is a coalition of 31 states, each with their own statewide network, that helps bring together policymakers, educators, youth development workers and others in an effort to improve outcomes for children and youth through school-based and school-linked after-school programs. Whatever the mechanism, the voice of principals, sharing authentic stories and needs, can help to raise awareness among governors, mayors and other decision makers about the impact—and potential—of after-school.

3. Advocate at all levels for adequate funding for after-school. These funds should supplement, not supplant, funds originally awarded for other education programs. Research shows that students who regularly participate in after-school programs for several years benefit the most. Yet stable funding is a problem both locally and at the state and national levels. There is no systemic state funding, and only poor or schools in need of improvement qualify for federal 21st Century Community Learning Centers funding. To sustain programs, funds are often cobbled together from a variety of sources. Schools need ongoing, reliable funding to increase the number of after-school programs and to ensure that all children who want it have access to high-quality programs. Funds for after-school programs should be awarded in time for program operators to plan for the most efficient use of these resources.

4. Continue to increase funding of 21st Century Community Learning Centers. The 21st CCLC program, part of the No Child Left Behind Act, is a key source of after-school funds. The program is an opportunity for students and their families to continue to learn new skills and discover new abilities after the school day has ended.

The focus of this program is the provision of expanded academic enrichment opportunities for children attending low-performing schools. In addition, 21st CCLC programs provide youth development activities, drug and violence prevention programs, technology education programs, art, music and recreation programs, counseling and character education to enhance the academic component of the program.

Unfortunately, the amounts appropriated for 21st CCLC each year remain far short of the annual levels authorized by No Child Left Behind. NAESP urges Congress to substantially increase 21st Century appropriations.

5. Ensure the quality of after-school staff. All personnel associated with after-school should exhibit a solid understanding of children and adolescent development. Background checks should be conducted to assure that all personnel are without criminal records.

6. Provide principals with high-quality, ongoing professional development on after-school issues. Federal, state and local education agencies should promote efforts to build the capacity of principals to ensure an understanding of the important linkages between school and after-school programs and provide resources and flexibility to consider a number of ways to help them connect learning opportunities in each.

7. Use supplemental services as an opportunity to provide a continuum of supports for students. Tutorial services and academic enrichment activities within No Child Left Behind are designed to help students meet local and state academic standards in subjects such as reading and math. Although they encounter challenges, there are several well-known after-school programs that have become supplemental education service providers. For many students, after-school programs are the places where they receive homework help or enrichment opportunities. Tutoring, whether one-or-one or with peers, may be a component of after-school programs, as may programs that focus on enrichment, service learning or other activities.

8. Conduct more research on after-school. After-school is an emerging field, and research on what constitutes quality in after-school programs is still somewhat limited. Issues of staffing, funding, transportation and curriculum are often not addressed in the research findings, providing a vague picture of the necessary infrastructure for quality after-school programs. We encourage universities, philanthropists and associations to expand research on these various areas of after-school. An important component of research is evaluation. After-school programs should be evaluated, and the results of the evaluations should be used to improve programs where needed as well as to make the case for increased funding and other types of support for after-school.

9. Link after-school programs to other social service programs in the community. After-school programs provide a flexible and appropriate environment to connect families with social service providers. After-school settings give providers access to parents whose work schedules may not permit them to visit school during the regular day. Integrating social services after school may give parents a better opportunity to access them when they pick up their children or participate in activities designed for families.

10. Recognize wellness and nutrition as important components in children's overall ability to learn. After-school programs must provide healthy snacks and, in some cases, dinner, particularly for low-income children. NAESP encourages the U.S. Department of Agriculture to provide resources for meals and snacks for participants in after-school programs. After-school can also play an important role in addressing issues such as obesity prevention by providing sports and recreational activities that supplement school-day physical education programs.

Methodology

Building on the release of two landmark publications that have made significant impact in informing and improving principal practice across the nation—*Leading Learning Communities: Standards for What Principals Should Know and Be Able To Do* in 2001 and *Leading Early Childhood Learning Communities* in 2004—the National Association of Elementary School Principals sought to continue its commitment to providing principals with the resources they need to expand the continuum of learning and help all children succeed.

Given this goal, NAESP called on the expertise of Collaborative Communications Group to conduct a rigorous examination of research; engage principals, researchers and individuals in professional organizations concerned with after-school; and write and design the newest guide for principals: *Leading After-School Learning Communities.* The eight-month process, begun in 2005, included:

Discovery interviews. Leaders in research, policy and practice provided significant perspective regarding NAESP's and principals' roles in the field of after-school. Interviews also provided context about important linkages between after-school programs and comprehensive child development.

Creating and convening an After-School Standards Committee. Principals were nominated to the committee based on their excellence in helping lead after-school programs in their schools and communities. These principals, along with individuals from after-school and other professional organizations, helped shape the guide through a review of research, as well as discussions and approval of the conceptual framework. The committee also provided examples of effective practice, which are featured throughout this guide.

Scholarly research. A review of relevant research spanned quality programming; local, state and federal policies; funding streams; youth development principles; program planning and evaluation; parent and community engagement; and staffing and professional development practices.

Interviews with principals. Conversations with elementary and middle school principals were centered around effective practices, the role of the principal in developing and supporting quality after-school programs and the role of NAESP as a continued supporter of quality after-school learning communities.

Discussion with the NAESP Board of Directors. A meeting with the NAESP Board of Directors provided an opportunity for reflection on the initial outline and fundamental messages of the guide.

Review of drafts. NAESP leadership and staff members, Standards Committee members and external peers in after-school and other professional organizations provided candid and invaluable feedback that helped to ensure the accuracy and credibility of this guide.

ACKNOWLEDGMENTS

NAESP gratefully acknowledges the individuals who contributed to the creation of this guide, including:

- The principals and representatives of professional organizations who participated on the Standards Committee, listed on the following page, for their insight, candor and leadership of after-school programs in their schools, cities and states. Also, Kanisha Williams-Jones, Senior Manager, Annual Conference Programming at the National School Boards Association, for her contributions at the initial meeting.

- The NAESP Board of Directors, for their commitment to progressive practice and quality learning opportunities for all children.

- External reviewers, including Priscilla Little, Harvard Family Research Project; Carol McElvain, Learning Point Associates; Terry Peterson, Afterschool and Community Learning Network; and Jane Quinn, the Children's Aid Society.

- The Charles Stewart Mott Foundation, for its continued dedication to establishing stable, quality after-school programming for children and youth and for supporting life-long learning opportunities for family and community members.

- Collaborative Communications Group staff and consultants, including Kris Kurtenbach and Terri Ferinde Dunham, Partners; John Gehring; Helen Janc Malone; Janalee Jordan-Meldrum; Meghan Neary; Robert Rothman; and Liz Worley. Art direction and design were provided by Bill Glover of the Design Partnership. Photographs by Bill Glover.

- NAESP staff members, for their commitment to providing research, professional development and expanded learning opportunities for elementary and middle school principals across the country, including:

  Vincent L. Ferrandino, Ed.D., Executive Director; Gail Connelly, Deputy Executive Director; Deborah B. Reeve, Ed.D., Deputy Executive Director; Cheryl Riggins, Ed.D., Associate Executive Director; Merrie Hahn, Senior Director, Programs; Lynn Hoffman, Administrative Assistant, Leadership Academy and Urban Alliances; Sally McConnell, Ph.D., Associate Executive Director, Government Relations; Raven Padgett, Director, Communications and Public Relations.

AFTER-SCHOOL STANDARDS COMMITTEE

Susan E. Masterson, Chair
President, NAESP Board of Directors
Monroe Elementary School
555 South Pontiac
Janesville, WI 53545

Tom Archuleta, Principal
Valdez Elementary School
2525 W. 29th Ave.
Denver, CO 80211

Tammy Condren, Principal
Marion C. Early School District
5309 S. Main
P.O. Box 96
Morrisville, MO 65710

Kathy Corley, Principal
Sara Harp Minter Elementary School
1650 Hwy. 85 South
Fayettesville, GA 30215

Pat Echanis, Principal
Parkdale Elementary School
P.O. Box 69
Parkdale, OR 97041

Donna Erwin, Principal
Four Georgians Elementary School
555 Custer
Helena, MT 59601

Jill Flanders, Principal
Plains Elementary School
267 Granby Road
South Hadley, MA 01075

Mary Grant, Principal
Takoma Education Center
7010 Piney Branch Road, NW
Washington, DC 20012

Janalee Jordan-Meldrum, Consultant
15 N. Irving Street
Arlington, VA 22201

Juli Kwikkel, Principal
East & West Elementary School
PO Box 638
419 Lake Ave.
Storm Lake, IA 50588

Carol Mitchell, Program Manager
21st Century Community Learning Centers
U.S. Department of Education
400 Maryland Ave., SW
Washington, DC 20202

Elizabeth Partoyan, Director
Research, Training and Member Services
National School Boards Association
1680 Duke Street
Alexandria, VA 22314

David Poer, Principal
Williamstown Elementary School
300 Helton St.
Williamstown, KY 41097

Margaret Scott, Principal
Fairview Elementary
5815 Ox Road
Fairfax Station, VA 22039

Bonnie Tryon, Principal
Golding Elementary School
177 Golding Drive
Cobleskill, NY 12043

Claudia Weisburd, Executive Director
Afterschool and Community Education
Foundations, Inc.
101 Executive Drive
Moorestown, NJ 08057

DISCOVERY INTERVIEWS

Martin Blank
Director for School, Family and Community Connections
Coalition for Community Schools,
Institute for Educational Leadership
Washington, DC

Sharon Deich
Program Manager
Community Systems Group
The Finance Project
Washington, DC

Ayeola Fortune
Project Director, Extended Learning
Council of Chief State School Officers
Washington, DC

Melissa Ganley
Program Manager
National PTA
Washington, DC

Jodi Grant
Executive Director
Afterschool Alliance
Washington, DC

Terry Peterson
Senior Fellow, University of South Carolina Foundation, and
Director, Afterschool and Community Learning Network
College of Education-Dean's Office
University of South Carolina
Columbia, SC

Jane Quinn
Assistant Executive Director for Community Schools
The Children's Aid Society
New York, NY

Carter Savage
Vice President, Youth Development, Program Services
Boys & Girls Clubs of America
Atlanta, GA

NAESP BOARD OF DIRECTORS

Bibliography

STANDARD ONE: Vision

Afterschool Alliance. *2004 Poll on Afterschool and Education.* Washington, DC: 2004.

Afterschool Alliance. *America After 3PM: A Household Survey on Afterschool in America.* Washington, DC: 2004.

Afterschool Alliance. *Here Is How You Can Help.* Washington, DC: 2004.

Afterschool Investments Project. *Creating a Vision for Afterschool Partnerships.* Washington, DC: U.S. Department of Health and Human Services, 2004.

Ashcraft, M. *Best Practices for School-Age Care Programs.* Santa Fe, NM: New Mexico Public Education Department, 2003.

The Annie E. Casey Foundation. *Success in School: Education Ideas That Count.* Baltimore, MD: 2005.

Bodilly, S. and Beckett, M. K. *Making Out-of-School Time Matter: Evidence for an Action Agenda.* Washington, DC: Rand Corporation, 2005.

Cohen, J. H. "Supplemental Education: Six Essential Components." *Principal, Beyond the Bell,* Vol. 82. No. 5. Alexandria, VA: May/June 2003.

Duffett, A. and Johnson, J. *All Work and No Play? Listening to What Kids and Parents Really Want From Out-of-School Time.* New York, NY: Public Agenda, 2004.

The Finance Project. *Creating a Vision for After School Partnerships.* Washington, DC: June 2004.

The Forum for Youth Investment. "Out-of-School Time and Civic Engagement." *Out-of-School Time Policy Commentary*, Issue 8. Washington, DC: October 2004.

Halpern, R. *Making Play Work: The Promise of After-School Programs for Low-Income Children.* New York: Teachers College Press, 2003.

Halpern, R., Spielberger, J. and Robb, S. *Making the Most of Out-of-School Time.* New York, NY: DeWitt Wallace-Reader's Digest Fund, December 1998.

Kail, R. (Ed.) "Out-of-School Settings as a Developmental Context for Children and Youth." *Advances in Child Development and Behavior*, Vol. 33. San Diego, CA: 2005.

Magnuson, P. "Extending the Day: School Programs Fill the Void Before and After-School." *Communicator.* Alexandria, VA: National Association of Elementary School Principals, March 2001.

McCloud, B. and Hale, B. "Preparing and Supporting School Principals." *The Mid-Atlantic Regional Educational Laboratory Field Notes.* Philadelphia, PA: Temple University, Spring 2005.

Murnane, R. and Levy, F. "Preparing Students To Thrive in 21st Century America: The Role for After-School." *Reimagining After-School: A Symposium on Learning and Leading in the 21st Century.* Cambridge, MA: Harvard Graduate School of Education, April 2004.

Murnane, R. and Levy, F. *Teaching the New Basic Skills.* New York, NY: Martin Kessler Books/The Free Press, 1996.

National Association of Elementary School Principals. "Principals and After-School Programs: A Survey of K-8 Principals." Fact sheet. Alexandria, VA: 2001.

National Education Commission on Time and Learning. *Prisoners of Time.* Washington, DC: U.S. Department of Education, 1994.

Noam, G. *New School-Burdened Principal.* Cambridge, MA: Harvard Graduate School of Education, 2002.

Noam, G., Biancarosa, G. and Dechausay, N. *Afterschool Education: Approaches to an Emerging Field.* Cambridge, MA: Harvard Graduate School of Education, 2002.

Peterson, T. "Leveraging the After-School Value Added." *The School Administrator.* Arlington, VA: American Association of School Administrators, May 2005.

Viadero, D. "A Cultural Odyssey." *Education Week.* Bethesda, MD: March 23, 2005.

U.S. Department of Education. *After-School Programs: Keeping Children Safe and Smart.* Washington, DC: 2000.

STANDARD TWO: Community Catalyst

Afterschool Alliance. "Afterschool, Community Service and Volunteerism." *Afterschool Alert Issue Brief,* No. 10. Washington, DC: August 2004.

Afterschool Alliance. "Afterschool Programs Strengthen Communities." *Afterschool Alert Issue Brief,* No. 18. Washington, DC: January 2004.

Afterschool Alliance. *Thirty-Five Ways State Education Agencies Can Build Public Understanding on Afterschool: Thoughts From the Field.* Washington, DC: undated.

Arts Education Partnership. *A Guide to Arts and Education Collaboration—Learning Partnerships: Improving Learning in Schools With Arts Partners in the Community.* Washington, DC: 1999.

Corporate Voices for Working Families. *After School for All: A Call to Action From the Business Community.* New York, NY: 2005.

Experience Corps. *Experience After School: Engaging Older Adults in After-School Programs.* Washington, DC: Civic Ventures, 2004.

Fagan, J. "Extended Learning for Children of Poverty," *Principal, Beyond the Bell,* Vol. 82, No. 5. Alexandria, VA: May/June 2003.

Fashola, O. "Implementing Effective After-School Programs." *Here's How,* Vol. 17. No. 3. Alexandria, VA: National Association of Elementary School Principals, March, 1999.

Ferguson, C. "Organizing Family and Community Connections With Schools: How Do School Staff Build Meaningful Relationships With All Stakeholders?" *A Strategic Brief of the National Center for Family and Community Connections With Schools.* Austin, TX: August 2005.

Ferguson, C. "Reaching Out to Diverse Populations: What Can Schools Do To Foster Family-School Connections?" *A Strategic Brief of the National Center for Family and Community Connections With Schools.* Austin, TX: September 2005.

Foundations, Inc. *Homework Zone Kit.* Moorestown, NJ: Foundations, Inc., undated.

Harris, E. and Wimer, C. "Engaging With Families in Out-of-School Time Learning." *Out-of-School Time Evaluation Snapshot,* No. 4. Cambridge, MA: Harvard Family Research Project, April 2004.

Harvey, B. and Shortt, J. *Working Together for Children and Families: A Community's Guide to Making the Most of Out-of-School Time.* Wellesley, MA: National Institute on Out-of-School Time, 2001.

Innovation Center for Community and Youth Development. *Creating Change: How Organizations Connect With Youth, Build Communities and Strengthen Themselves.* Takoma Park, MD: 2003.

Innovation Center for Community and Youth Development. *Lessons in Leadership: How Young People Change Their Communities and Themselves.* Takoma Park, MD: 2004.

Innovation Center for Community and Youth Development. *Making the Case for Youth in Decision-Making.* Takoma Park, MD: 2001.

Iowa Afterschool Alliance. *A Guide for Afterschool Community Forums.* Des Moines, IA: 2005.

Jehl, J., Blank, M. and McCloud, B. *Education and Community Building: Connecting the Two Worlds.* Washington, DC: Institute for Educational Leadership, 2001.

Kaplan, C. *Opening Doors for Boston's Children: Lessons Learned in Expanding School-Based After-School Programs.* Boston, MA: Boston's After-School for All Partnership, October 2004.

National Afterschool and Community Learning Network. "Afterschool and Summer Programs." *Occasional Paper Four.* Charleston, SC: Winter 2005-06.

National Association of Elementary School Principals. "Implementing Effective After-School Programs." *Here's How.* Vol. 7. No. 3. Alexandria, VA: March 1999.

National Coalition for Youth. "Research Tells Us: Partnership Between Schools and Community-Based Organizations Are Crucial." *Partnerships for After-School Success.* Washington, DC: February 2004.

National Collaboration for Youth/Coalition for Community Schools/Institute for Educational Leadership. *Helping Young People Succeed.* Washington, DC: undated.

Noam, G. "Afterschool Time: Towards a Theory of Collaborations." *Urban Seminar Series on Children's Mental Health and Safety: Out-of-School Time.* Boston, MA: May 2001.

Peterson, T. "Engaging and Enriching Afterschool Programs Through Statewide and Local Partnerships: Giving Children and Youth the Opportunities and Connections To Keep Them on Track." Remarks for NC-CAP Regional Meetings in Asheville and Winston-Salem, NC. Charleston, SC: Afterschool and Community Learning Network, November 2003.

Policy Studies Associates. "Collaborating With Principals in After-School Programs." *A TASC Brief.* Washington, DC: September 2000.

Polman, J., et al. "Youth Programs in the Community Context." *Afterschool Matters,* No. 3. New York, NY: Spring 2004.

Southwest Educational Developmental Laboratory. "Family and Community Connections With Schools." *SEDLetter,* Vol. 14. No. 1. Austin, TX: February 2002.

Southwest Educational Developmental Laboratory. "Learning Outside of the School Classroom: What Teachers Can Do To Involve Family in Supporting Classroom Instruction." *A Strategic Brief of the National Center for Family and Community Connections With Schools.* Austin, TX: September 2004.

Weiss, A. R. and Brigham, R. A. *The Family Participation in After-School Study.* Boston, MA: Institute for Responsive Education, 2003.

Whalen, S. P. *Report of the Evaluation of the Polk Bros. Foundation Full Service School Initiative.* Chicago, IL: University of Chicago, April 2002.

STANDARD THREE: Infrastructure

Afterschool Alliance. *Working Families and Afterschool: A Special Report From America After 3PM.* Washington, DC: 2004.

Bagby, J. H. *A Resource Guide for Planning and Operating After-School Programs* (2nd Ed.). Austin, TX: Southwest Educational Development Laboratory, 2004.

Borden, L. M. "What Do Youth Say About Participation and Why We Need To Know." Presented at the Harvard Family Research Project After School Evaluation Symposium. Cambridge, MA: September 2005.

Caplan, J. and Calfee, C. *Strengthening Connections Between Schools and After-School Programs.* Chicago, IL: Learning Point Associates, 1998.

DeArmond, M., Taggart, S. and Hill, P. *The Future of School Facilities: Getting Ahead of the Curve.* Seattle, WA: Center for Reinventing Public Education, 2002.

Fight Crime: Invest in Kids. *Survey of American Working Mothers: Attitudes About Risks to Children as They Head Back to School.* Washington, DC: 2003.

The Finance Project. "Creating Dedicated Local Revenue Sources for Out-of-School Time Initiatives." *Strategy Brief,* Vol. 1. Washington, DC: September 1999.

The Finance Project. "Finding Resources to Support Rural Out-of-School Time Initiatives." *Strategy Brief,* Vol. 4. No. 1. Washington, DC: February 2003.

Lauer, R. "After-School Programs: Everybody's Doing It." *Principal, Beyond the Bell,* Vol. 82, No. 5. Alexandria, VA: May/June 2003.

Learning Point Associates. *Beyond the Bell: A Principal's Guide to Effective Afterschool Programs.* Chicago, IL: 2005.

Miller, B. M. *Critical Hours: Afterschool Programs and Educational Success.* Brookline, MA: Miller Midzik Research Associates, 2003.

National Institute on Out-of-School Time and the Academy for Educational Development Center for Youth Development and Policy Research. *Strategic Plan: Building a Skilled and Stable Out-of-School Time Workforce.* Wellesley, MA: 2003.

Newman, S., Fox, J., Flynn, E. and Christeson, W. *America's After-School Choice: The Prime Time for Juvenile Crime or Youth Enrichment and Achievement.* Washington, DC: Fight Crime: Invest in Kids, 2000.

Ouellette, M. *Extra Learning Opportunities That Encourage Healthy Lifestyles.* Washington, DC: Education Policy Studies, 2000.

Paisano-Trujillo, R. "Out-of-School Time: A Critical Setting for Promoting Positive Youth Development." Presented at the Harvard Family Research Project After School Evaluation Symposium. Cambridge, MA: September 2005.

Policy Studies Associates. "After-School Homework Help." *A TASC Brief.* Washington, DC: May 2001.

Policy Studies Associates. *Building the Skills of After-School Staff: A Tool Kit.* Washington, DC: 2000.

Rinehart, J. "A Principal's Fulfilled Vision." *Principal, Beyond the Bell,* Vol. 82, No. 5. Alexandria, VA: May/June 2003.

Surr, W. B. "New Roles Are Emerging: Will Practitioners Soon Have a More Expanded Career Menu?" *Emerging Roles in the Field,* Issue 3. Wellesley, MA: June 2001.

Waters, T., Marzano, R. and McNulty, B. *Balanced Leadership: What 30 Years of Research Tells Us About the Effect of Leadership on Student Achievement.* Aurora, CO: Mid-continent Research for Education and Learning, 2003.

Wimer, C., Post, M. and Little, P. "Leveraging Resources To Promote Positive School-CBO Relationships." *Afterschool Matters,* No. 3. New York, NY: Spring 2004.

STANDARD FOUR: Quality Content

Afterschool Alliance. "Afterschool Programs Meet the Needs of Youth in Rural America." *Issue Brief,* No. 4. Washington, DC: Afterschool Alliance, August 2004.

Arts Education Partnership. *Creating Quality Integrated and Interdisciplinary Arts Programs.* Washington, DC: 2002.

Bouffard, S. and Little, P. "Promoting Quality Through Professional Development: A Framework for Evaluation." *Issue and Opportunities in Out-of-School Time Evaluation,* No. 8. Cambridge, MA: Harvard Family Research Project, August 2004.

Britsch, B., Martin, N., Stuczynski, A., Tomala, B. and Tucci, P. *Literacy in Afterschool Programs: Literature Review.* Austin, TX: National Partnership for Quality Afterschool Learning, 2005.

Chung, A. *After-School Programs: Keeping Children Safe and Smart.* Washington, DC: U.S. Department of Education, 2000.

Colorado Foundation for Families and Children. *After School Programming: A Pressing Need and a Public Priority* (4th Ed.). Denver, CO: 2004.

Cooper, H. M. *The Battle Over Homework: Common Ground for Administrators, Teachers and Parents* (2nd Ed.). Thousand Oaks, CA: Corwin Press, 2001.

Council of Chief State School Officers. *Summer Learning Opportunities in High-Poverty Schools.* Washington, DC: 2005.

Daughtry, G. "Building a Professional Development System Through Standards." Presented at the Harvard Family Research Project After School Evaluation Symposium. Cambridge, MA: September 2005.

Doolittle, F. "Testing Enhanced Academic Instruction in After-School Programs." Presented at the Harvard Family Research Project After School Evaluation Symposium. Cambridge, MA: September 2005.

The Forum for Youth Investment. "Inside the Black Box: Exploring the Content of After-School." *Out-of-School Time Policy Commentary*, Issue 5. Washington, DC: November 2003.

The Forum for Youth Investment. "School's Out: A Look at Summer Learning and Engagement." *Out-of-School Time Policy Commentary*, Issue 7. Washington, DC: July 2004.

Gardner, H. *Multiple Intelligences: The Theory in Practice.* New York, NY: Basic Books, 1993.

Grossman, J. Price, M., Fellerath, V., Jucovy, L., Kotloff, L., Raley, R. and Walker, K. *Multiple Choices After School: Findings From the Extended-Service School Initiative.* Philadelphia, PA: Public/Private Ventures, 2002.

Hall, G., Yohalem, N., Tolman, J. and Wilson, A. *How Afterschool Programs Can Most Effectively Promote Positive Youth Development as a Support to Academic Achievement.* Wellesley, MA: National Institute on Out-of-School Time, 2003.

Harvard Family Research Project. "Evaluation Out-of-School Time Program Quality." *The Evaluation Exchange*, Vol. 10. No. 1. Cambridge, MA: Spring 2004.

Haugenbrook, A. K. "Developing and Evaluation Professional Development Efforts for After School: A Practice Perspective from Citizen Schools." Presented at the Harvard Family Research Project After School Evaluation Symposium. Cambridge, MA: September 2005.

Hepburn, K. S. *Building Culturally & Linguistically Complete Services To Support Young Children, Their Families, and School Readiness.* Baltimore, MD: The Annie E. Casey Foundation, 2004.

Jordan-Meldrum, J. *Making the Most of After-School Time: Ten Case Studies of School-Based After-School Programs.* Alexandria, VA: National Association of Elementary School Principals, 2005.

Kansas Enrichment Network. *A Call for Quality Afterschool Programs in Kansas.* Lawrence, KS: October 2004.

Lauer, P., Akiba, M., Wilkerson, S., Apthorp, H., Snow, D. and Martin-Glenn, M. *The Effectiveness of Out-of-School-Time Strategies in Assisting Low-Achieving Students in Reading and Mathematics.* Washington, DC: U.S. Department of Education, 2004.

Lauer, R. "Understanding the Research: Making the Case for Quality Summer Learning Programs." Presented at the Beyond School Hours VIII: The Power of Partnerships. Atlanta, GA: February 2005.

National Collaboration for Youth. "Research Tells Us: All Youth Deserve High-Quality After-School Programming." *Partnership for After-School Success.* Washington, DC: February 2004.

National Institute on Out-of-School Time. *Discovering Community: Activities for Afterschool Programs.* Wellesley, MA: 2004.

National Institute on Out-of-School Time. "From Contrast to Concrete: Issues in Building a Skilled and Stable Out-of-School Time Workforce." *After School Issues.* Wellesley, MA: June 2001.

New York State Afterschool Network. *Program Quality Self-Assessment Tool: Planning for Ongoing Program Improvement.* New York, NY: January 2005.

Noam, G. "After-School Education: What Principals Should Know." *Principal, Beyond the Bell,* Vol. 82. No. 5. Alexandria, VA: May/June 2003.

Policy Studies Associates. "Identifying Staffing Needs and Recruiting Qualified After-School Staff." *A TASC Resource Brief.* Washington, DC: October 2000.

Policy Studies Associates. *What Does Prior Research Suggest Regarding Essential Program Features Associated With After-School Quality?* Washington, DC: undated.

Quinn, Jane. *How Do After-School Programs Contribute to Young People's Academic Success?* New York, NY: The Children's Aid Society, undated.

Reisner, E., White, R., Russell, C. and Birmingham, J. *Building Quality, Scale and Effectiveness in After-School Programs.* Washington, DC: Policy Studies Associates, 2004.

Save the Children Federation. *Recipes for Success: Promising Practices From Rural Afterschool Programs.* Westport, CT: Save the Children Federation, 2003.

Vandell, D. L. "What We Know and What We Need To Know To Improve Program Quality." Presented at the Harvard Family Research Project After School Evaluation Symposium. Cambridge, MA: September 2005.

The Wallace Foundation. *Quality That Lasts: Building a Framework for the Future of OST.* Washington, DC: 2005.

Weisburd, C., Adorno, S. and Lauer, R. *Academic Content, After-School Style: A Notebook and Guide.* Moorestown, NJ: Foundations, Inc., 2004.

STANDARD FIVE: Evaluation

Afterschool Alliance. "Formal Evaluations of the Academic Impact of Afterschool Programs." *Afterschool Alliance Backgrounder.* Washington, DC: September 2004.

Afterschool Alliance. "Formal Evaluations of the Academic Impact of Behavior, Safety and Family Life." *Afterschool Alliance Backgrounder.* Washington, DC: March 2004.

American Association of School Administrators. "After-school Hours." *School Governance and Leadership.* Arlington, VA: May 2005.

Bell, M. "Are After-School Programs Accountable?" *Principal, Beyond the Bell.* Vol. 82, No. 5. Alexandria, VA: May/June 2003.

Bouffard, S. and Little, P. "Detangling Data Collection: Methods for Gathering Data." *Out-of-School Time Evaluation Snapshot.* No. 5. Cambridge, MA: Harvard Family Research Project, August 2004.

C. S. Mott Foundation Committee on After-School Research and Practice. *Moving Towards Success: Framework for After-School Programs.* Washington, DC: Collaborative Communications Group, 2005.

Center for Applied Research and Evaluation, University of Minnesota. *Final Evaluation Report: 21st Century Community Learning Centers Pathways to Progress, St. Paul Public Schools.* Minneapolis, MN: March 2004.

Dynarski, M., James-Burdumy, S., Moore, M., Rosenberg, L., Deke, J. and Mansfield, W. *When Schools Stay Open Late: The National Evaluation of the 21st Century Community Learning Centers Program.* Washington, DC: U.S. Department of Education, 2004.

Fiester, L. *Afterschool Counts! A Guide to Issue and Strategies for Monitoring Attendance in Afterschool and Other Youth Programs.* Washington, DC: Policy Studies Associates, undated.

Harvard Family Research Project. "Why, When and How To Use Evaluation." *Issues and Opportunities in Out-of-School Time Evaluation*, No. 5. Cambridge, MA: June 2003.

Intercultural Center for Research in Education and National Institute on Out-of-School Time. *Pathways to Success for Youth: What Counts in After-School.* Arlington, MA: November 2005.

Le Menestrel, S. "Promising Practices in After-School: Creating Engaging Learning Environments for Children and Youth." Presented at Beyond School Hours VII: Viewing Challenges as Opportunities. San Diego, CA: February 2004.

Lewis, A. and Paik, S. *Add It Up: Using Research To Improve Education for Low-Income and Minority Students.* Washington, DC: Poverty & Race Research Action Council, 2001.

Little, P. *Large Scale Evaluations.* Cambridge, MA: Harvard Family Research Project, September 2005.

Little, P. *Selected Evaluation Terms.* Cambridge, MA: Harvard Family Research Project, March 2002.

Little, P., DuPree, S. and Deich, S. *Documenting Progress and Demonstrating Results: Evaluating Local Out-of-School Time Programs.* Cambridge, MA: Harvard Family Research Project, 2002.

Owens, D. "Eight Keys to a Successful Expanded Day Program." *Principal, Beyond the Bell*, Vol. 82, No. 5. Alexandria, VA: May/June 2003.

Reisner, E. R. *Using Evaluation Methods To Promote Continuous Improvement and Accountability in After-School Programs: A Guide.* Washington, DC: Policy Studies Associates, 2004.

Turino, H. (Ed.) "Dialogues in Philosophy, Practice and Evaluation." *Afterschool Matters*, Vol. 1. No. 1. New York, NY: Spring 2000.

Turnbull, B. J. and Smith, D. L. *Experience Corps in Urban Elementary Schools: A Survey of Principals.* Washington, DC: Policy Studies Associates, 2004.

Vandell, D. L., Reisner, E. R., Brown, B. B., Pierce, K. M., Dadisman, K. and Pechman, E. M. *The Study of Promising After-School Programs: Descriptive Report of the Promising Programs.* Washington, DC: Policy Studies Associates, undated.

Weinbaum, A. *Participant Assessment in Afterschool Programs.* New York, NY: Academy for Educational Development, 1996.

STANDARD SIX: Champion After-School

American Association of School Administrators. "Afterschool Programs: Bureaucratic Barriers and Strategies for Success." *School Governance and Leadership.* Arlington, VA: Fall 2005.

Belden, N., Russonello J. and Stewart, K. *School Board Presidents' Views of After-School Programs in American Schools: Results of Survey Research Conducted for the National School Boards Association.* Alexandria, VA: National School Boards Association, May 2003.

Council of Chief State School Officers. *Using NCLB Funds To Support Extended Learning Time: Opportunities for Afterschool Programs.* Washington, DC: 2005.

Deich, S., Wegener, V. and Wright, E. "Using Title I To Support Out-of-School Time and Community School Initiatives." *Strategy Brief,* Vol. 2. No. 4. Washington, DC: The Finance Project, January 2002.

Ferber, T., Gaines, E. and Goodman, C. "Positive Youth Development: State Strategies." *Strengthening Youth Policy.* Washington, DC: National Conference of State Legislatures, October 2005.

The Finance Project. "Sustaining Comprehensive Community Initiatives: Key Elements for Success." *Financing Strategy Brief.* Washington, DC: April, 2002.

The Forum for Youth Investment. "After-School for All? Exploring Access and Equity in After-School Programs." *Out-of-School Time Policy Commentary,* Issue 4. Washington, DC: July 2003.

Hall, G. and Harvey, B. *Building and Sustaining Citywide Afterschool Initiatives – Experiences of the Cross-Cities Network Citywide Afterschool Initiatives.* Wellesley, MA: National Institute on Out-of-School Time, November 2002.

Hutchinson, A. and Van Wyngaardt, D. *Stronger Schools, Stronger Cities.* Washington, DC: National League of Cities, 2004.

Landford, B. H. *Cost Worksheet for Out-of-School Time and Community School Initiatives.* Washington, DC: The Finance Project, 2000.

Lauver, S. and Little, P. "Finding the Right Hook: Strategies for Attracting and Sustaining Participation in After-School Programs." *The School Administrator.* Arlington, VA: American Association of School Administrators, May 2005.

Lauver, S., Little, P. and Weiss, H. "Moving Beyond the Barriers." *Issues and Opportunities in Out-of-School Time Evaluation,* No. 6. Cambridge, MA: Harvard Family Research Project, July 2004.

National Center for Community Education. *Fact Sheets for Afterschool Funding.* Flint, MI: undated.

National Center for Community Education. *Public Policy Makers.* Flint, MI: undated.

National School Boards Association. *Building and Sustaining After-School Programs: Successful Practices in School Board Leadership.* Alexandria, VA: 2005.

Peterson, T. and Spitz, C. "Sustaining Afterschool Programs." *Community Education Journal*, Vol. 29. No. 3/4. Fairfax, VA: National Community Education Association, Spring/Summer 2002.

Peterson, T. and Owens, D. "Strategies for Sustaining Afterschool Programs." Prepared for the National Elementary School Principals Annual Convention. San Francisco, CA: April 2004.

Policy Studies Associates. *Sustainability in School-Linked After-School Programs.* Washington, DC: 2002.

Rinehart, J. "A New Day Begins After-School." *Principal, Beyond the Bell*, Vol. 82, No. 5. Alexandria, VA: May/June 2003.

Southwest Educational Development Laboratory. *Making the Most of the Connection: A Policymaker's Guide to Participating in a Community Dialogue on Education.* Austin, TX: 2000.

Tolman, J., Pittman, K., Yohalem, N., Thomases, J. and Trammel, M. *Moving an Out-of-School Agenda: Lessons and Challenges Across Cities.* New York, NY: The Forum for Youth Investment, 2002.

Washington Afterschool Network. *Afterschool in Washington: A Smart, Strategic Investment.* Seattle, WA: December 2004.

Wright, E. and Deich, S. *Replacing Initial Grants: Tips for Out-of-School Time Programs and Initiatives.* Washington, DC: The Finance Project, December 2002.

NOTES

NOTES

NOTES

NOTES